The ✳ COSMIC JOURNAL

Also by Yanik Silver

Evolved Enterprise

Maverick Startup

Hay House Titles of Related Interest

YOU CAN HEAL YOUR LIFE, the movie,
starring Louise Hay & Friends
(available as a 1-DVD program, an expanded 2-DVD set,
and an online streaming video)
Watch the trailer at: www.hayhouse.com/louise-movie

THE SHIFT, the movie, starring Dr. Wayne W. Dyer
(available as a 1-DVD program, an expanded 2-DVD set,
and on online streaming video)
Watch the trailer at: www.hayhouse.com/the-shift-movie

*Change Your Thoughts—Change Your Life: Living the
Wisdom of the Tao,* by Dr. Wayne W. Dyer

*Life on Earth: Understanding Who We Are,
How We Got Here, and What May Lie Ahead,*
by Mike Dooley

*Trust Life: Love Yourself Every Day with Wisdom
from Louise Hay,* by Louise Hay

Please visit:

Hay House USA: www.hayhouse.com®
Hay House Australia: www.hayhouse.com.au
Hay House UK: www.hayhouse.co.uk
Hay House India: www.hayhouse.co.in

The COSMIC JOURNAL

Yanik Silver

HAY HOUSE, INC.
Carlsbad, California • New York City
London • Sydney • New Delhi

Published in the United States by: Hay House, Inc.: www.hayhouse.com®
• *Published in Australia by:* HayHouse Australia Pty. Ltd.: www.hayhouse.com
.au • *Published in the United Kingdom by:* Hay House UK, Ltd.: www.hayhouse
.co.uk • *Published in India by:* Hay House Publishers India: www.hayhouse.co.in

Cover design: Micah Kandros • *Interior design:* Jessica Angerstein • *Interior
layout:* Nick C. Welch • *Illustrations by:* Yanik Silver

Page 19 "You Cannot Have Within You…": Rumi quote, "What you seek is also
seeking you." Copyright © Coleman Barks, used by permission of the author-
translator.

Page 37 "Joy Is Your Soul's GPS": Lyrics, "That which you adore is the key to the
door" from "Temples" from the album *Ritual Mystic* by MC YOGI. Copyright © 2016
MC YOGI, used by permission of the artist.

Page 69 "There Is a Crack in Everything… That's How the Light Gets In": Lyrics
from "Anthem" by Leonard Cohen. Copyright © 1993 by Leonard Cohen and
Leonard Cohen Stranger Music, Inc., used by permission of The Wylie Agency LLC.

Page 71 "Celebrate Mistakes": Illustration of stop sign was inspired by "Celebrate
Mistakes" by Scott Froschauer, www.scottfroschauer.com. Copyright © 2017 by
Scott Froschauer, used by permission of the artist.

Page 99 "Love Spray": Illustration of spray can was inspired by "Lovespray"
by Con$umr, www.artbyconsumer.com. Copyright © 2016 by Con$umr, used by
permission of the artist.

Page 107 "Doors Will Open for You Where There Were Only Walls": Illustration of
door was inspired by "Follow Your Bliss" by Jennifer Verge, www.jenniferverge
.com. Copyright © 2013 by Jennifer Verge, used by permission of the artist.

Page 137 "See with Your Soul's Eyes": Rumi quote, "Close both eyes to see
with the other eye." Copyright © Coleman Barks, used by permission of the
author-translator.

Page 189 "Welcome to the Ascending Silver Age": Yuga diagram based on the
work of Walter Cruttenden and Swami Sri Yukteswar's *The Holy Science.* Used by
permission of Walter Cruttenden.
Lyrics from "We Are on Time" by Nahko And Medicine For The People. Copyright
© 2016 Medicine For The People Music, used by permission of the artist.

The author of this book does not dispense medical advice or prescribe
the use of any technique as a form of treatment for physical, emotional,
or medical problems without the advice of a physician, either directly or
indirectly. The intent of the author is only to offer information of a general
nature to help you in your quest for emotional, physical, and spiritual well-
being. In the event you use any of the information in this book for yourself,
the author and the publisher assume no responsibility for your actions.

Library of Congress Control Number: 2019947530

Tradepaper ISBN: 978-1-4019-5913-5

10 9 8 7 6 5 4 3 2 1
1st edition, November 2019

Printed in the United States of America

SUSTAINABLE
FORESTRY
INITIATIVE
Certified Chain of Custody
Promoting Sustainable Forestry
www.sfiprogram.org
SFI-01268
SFI label applies to the text stock

" *To Catalyze the Cosmos*
In Service of ONE "

This book belongs to

Name: _____

If found
please read
3 entries and
Then return.

- REWARD -

ph: _____
e: _____

You made it!

Here it IS - the journal you wrote for yourself. Your Galactic Instruction Manual you were missing at birth to Re-remember WHO you are and what the heck you're doing here... at this time. It's no accident you have the journal in your hands now. You set your own Cosmic Alarm Clock to go off and strike at exactly the appointed hour.

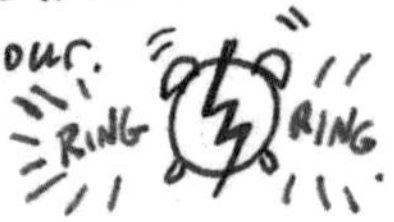
RING
RING

The Cosmic Journal is yours to use anyway you like. Read it one page at a time - or, even more powerful, is to use it like an oracle. Breathe deeply and hold your question or intention in mind, then flip to a page at "random" to see the perfect message awaiting you.

Write in it, embellish it, jot notes to yourself and even slip items inside your book to make it uniquely yours. The more you PLAY with it, the more you'll find the signs, symbols and synchronicities that are like magical keys that open doors for you.

Allow yourself to pen your own future, past and present in these pages. To connect your head, heart and highest purpose. Journaling is your journey to your NEXT greatest work here on this planet. And right now we need you more than ever to step up fully.

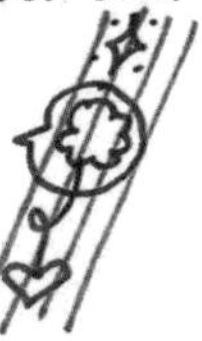

TRUST the Universe has even more in store for you than you can IMAGINE. Set your highest intention + hold on for the ride...

-Y.S.

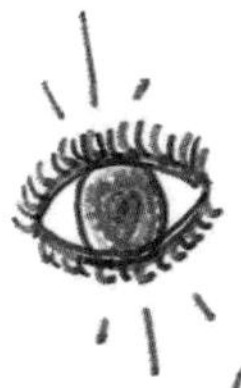

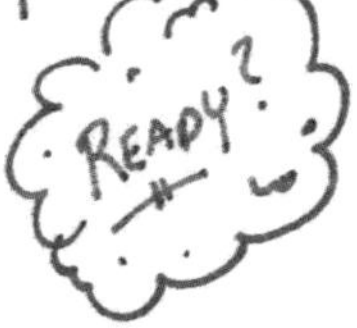
READY?

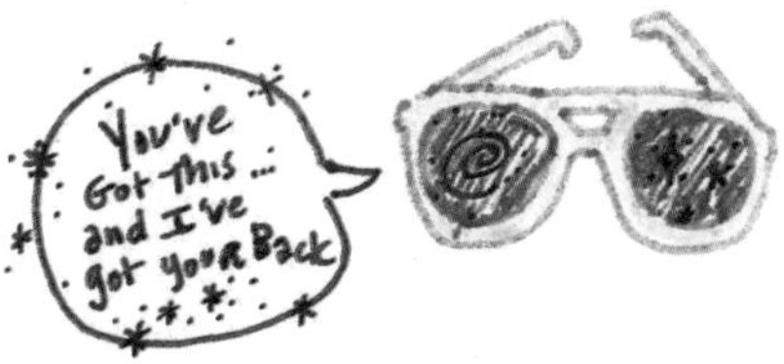
You've Got this... and I've Got your Back

INSTRUCTIONS: *Lucky Roll*

Let it Roll...

If you see This Icon, 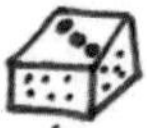 get your dice out to roll

You can play This game with any entry in This book

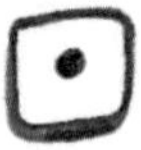 What is The ONE big Idea That jumps out at you in This entry?

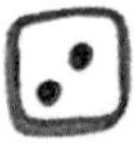 Meditate for 2 minutes. Now find one of your favorite books and turn to page 22 or 222. (or just flip to any page) How does This connect?

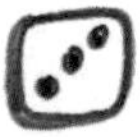 Past/Present/Future. How would your past versions present version and future version of yourself speak to This entry?

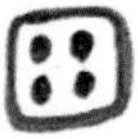 Go back 4 images in your phone. How does This connect? Draw it! (Don't worry, nobody is grading you)

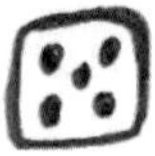 Have a Q+A dialogue with your cosmic self. Use your non-dominant hand to answer as The Universe

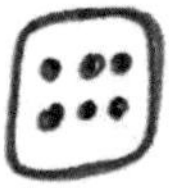 Six represents perfect structure. What is perfect about your situation right now? How does The entry remind you of The perfection of now?

Remember you can always make up your own rules or create your own version. And you don't even need to wait for The dice icon to roll.

xo

TRUST

TRUST THE UNIVERSE HAS EVEN MORE ☀
☀ IN STORE FOR YOU THAN YOU CAN IMAGINE...

· Trust your divine timing...
· Trust your crazy ideas...
· Trust your wings will grow when you leap...
· Trust your nature...
· Trust you've been encoded with a cosmic ALARM CLOCK...
· Trust the signs, symbols & synchronicities... ⏰
· Trust the co-conspirators catalyzing your evolution...
· Trust the perfect unfolding of your understanding...
· Trust your divine connection

— Necker Island, BVI, 6:10AM
(Sunrise)

EL SOÑADOR Y LO SOÑADO

3

ONE 1

One is the whole, never broken, the MONAD.
The original source, from which everything else springs forth. Just like white light contains the entire rainbow of colors. It's the beginning, our origination point.

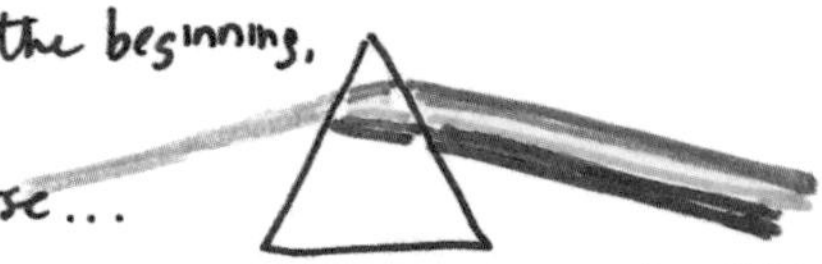

The start for the Universe...
Uni meaning one and the verse of this song to sound.
Our planets revolve around the ONE... And then our GALAXY revolves around the ONE central sun.

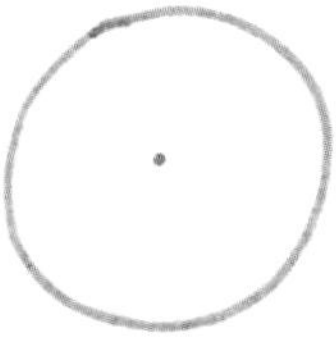

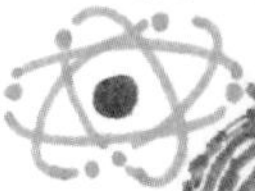

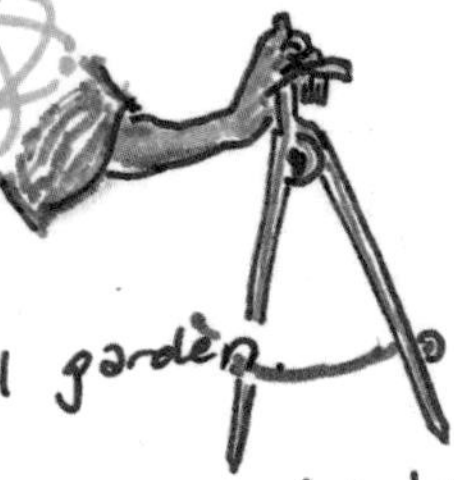

One is the seed blooming into a full garden.
One is our interconnected OCEAN.
One is the singular consciousness of LOVE. Not love like a husband + wife or two people together or even a child + parent, All of it and much more. Love is the ONE Universal force of attraction and allurement. Magically holding the elements together, bringing the right people into your life, your greatest work revealing itself to you.
Many mystics have said there is just ONE of us here. What I do to you, I do to myself. What I do to the Earth, I do to myself. There is just ONE of us here...

PLAYING AN INFINITE GAME of COSMIC
PEEK-A-BOO!! HIDE & SEEK

Ultimately returning to the ONE... in RE/UNION until the cycle starts again in the single BANG over and over again...

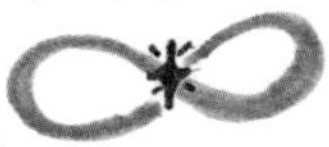

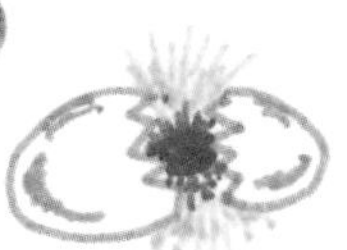

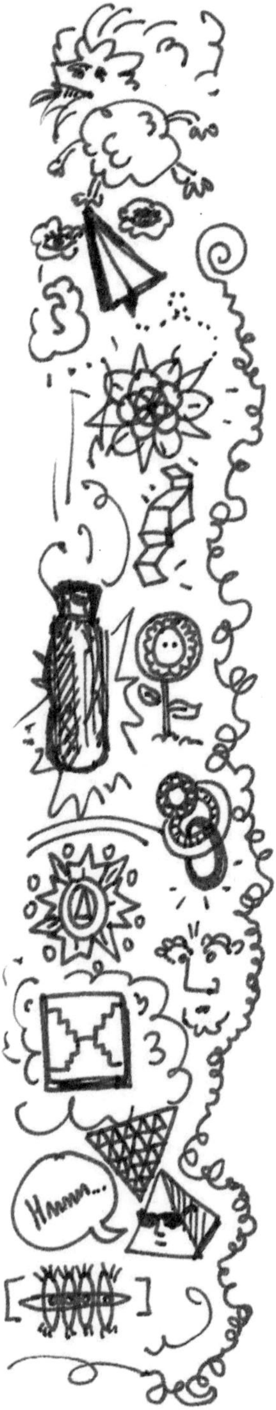
Hmmm...

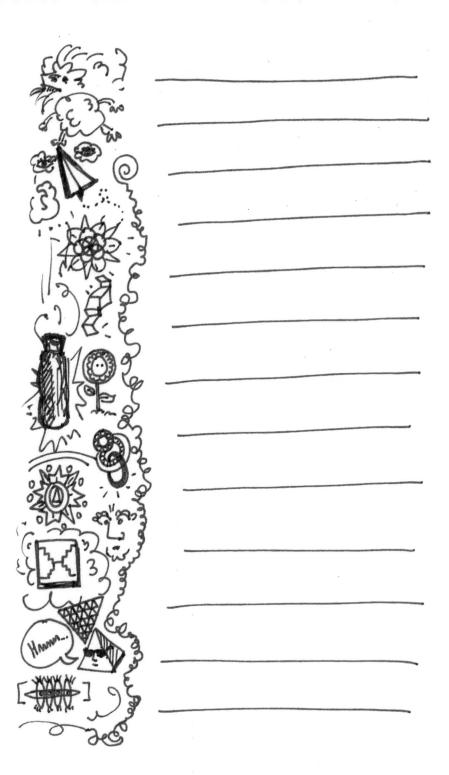

ONE DROP
IS STILL
PART of
THE WHOLE

You can never become separate from source just like
a drop of water cannot be apart from its ocean.
The drops always contains a perfect piece of where it
came from and will return to. But when the drop returns,
it also carries the experience and intelligence of new
learnings. The Ocean instantly evolves - just as all the drops.
We are able to know ourselves as a drop but not allow
that to be where we end. We are as big as the ocean
and then the Ocean is but one drop in the cosmic SEA. ✳
One within another... within another... and another... and so it
goes until we finally realize to love one single tiny drop is to
love everything all together.

The Universe Winks into Existence
Stars formed
Galaxies Collide
Universe is fine-tuned for life. If one tiny variable is off, everything would be nonexistent
Blah... Blah... Science Stuff
WELCOME EARTH

I'm on a roll... how about you?

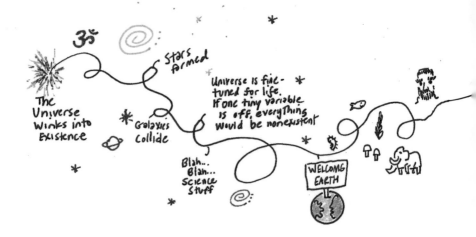

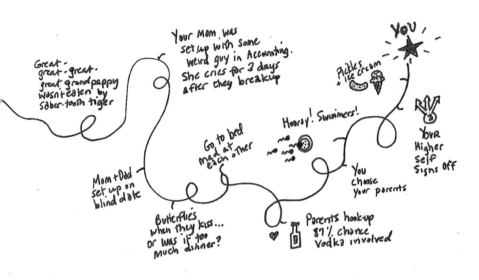

Great-great-great-great grandpappy wasn't eaten by saber-tooth tiger
Your Mom was set up with some weird guy in Accounting. She cries for 3 days after they breakup
YOU
Pickles + ice cream
Your Higher Self Signs off
Hooray! Swimmers!
Go to bed mad at each other
Mom + Dad set up on blind date
You choose your parents
Butterflies when they kiss... or was it too much dinner?
Parents hook-up 87% chance Vodka involved

You Already Won

The Cosmic Lottery

Imagine the mind-boggling and wondrous events, circumstances + synchronicities that had to occur in just the right order and the perfect way for You. The You that is perfectly designed for this moment in time + space for your purpose here. Provide your unique piece of the cosmic mosaic, the tapestry you add your design to. When you were born you were already encoded with the symbols, signs, colors, people, experiences, "coincidences," songs & ideas that would nudge you towards your true PATH. The Universe wouldn't go through all the trouble of having you if there wasn't a reason. Simply existing is worthy of LOVE + awe + gratitude. Now what you do with all your gifts, talents + resources is up to you. The Universe is calling to you to BE the channel for co-creating an evolution in consciousness and greater expansion...

A co-conspirator & playmate...

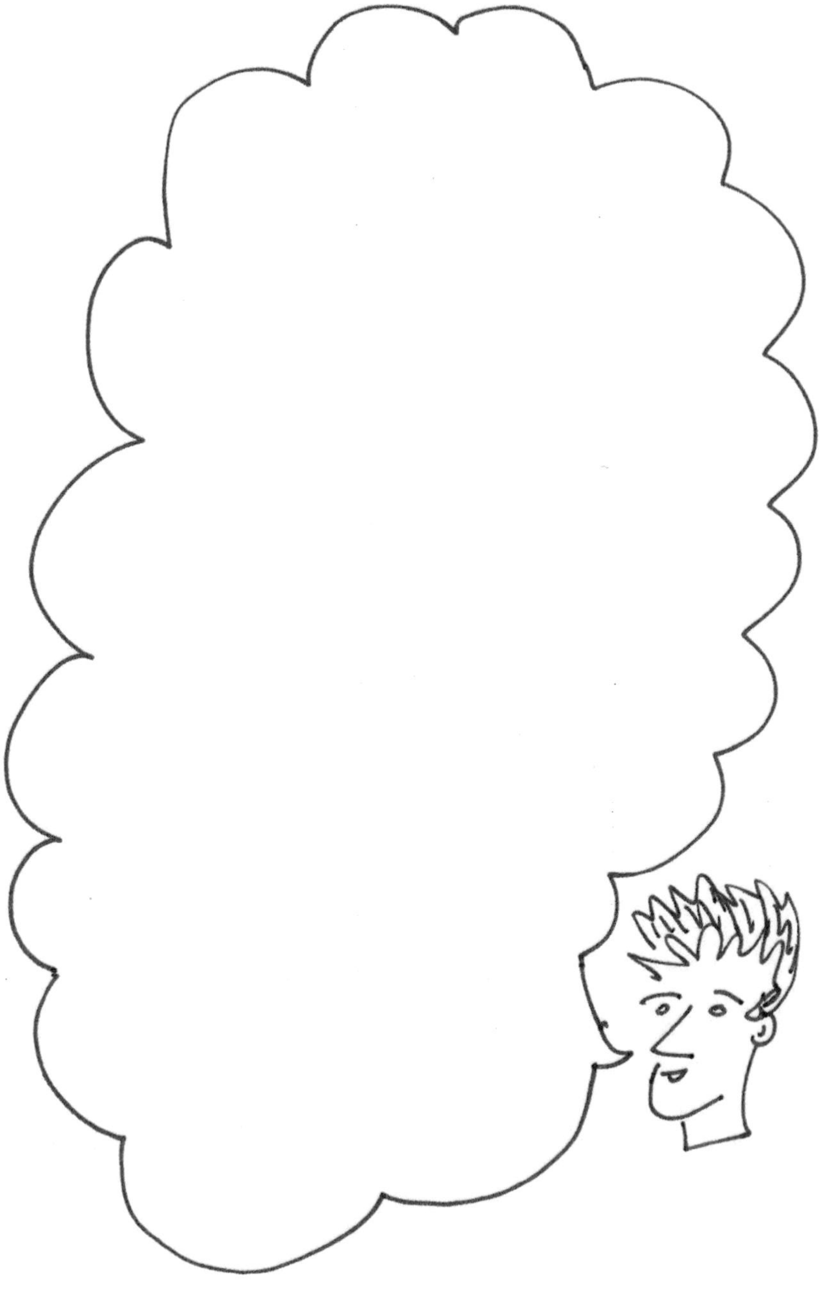

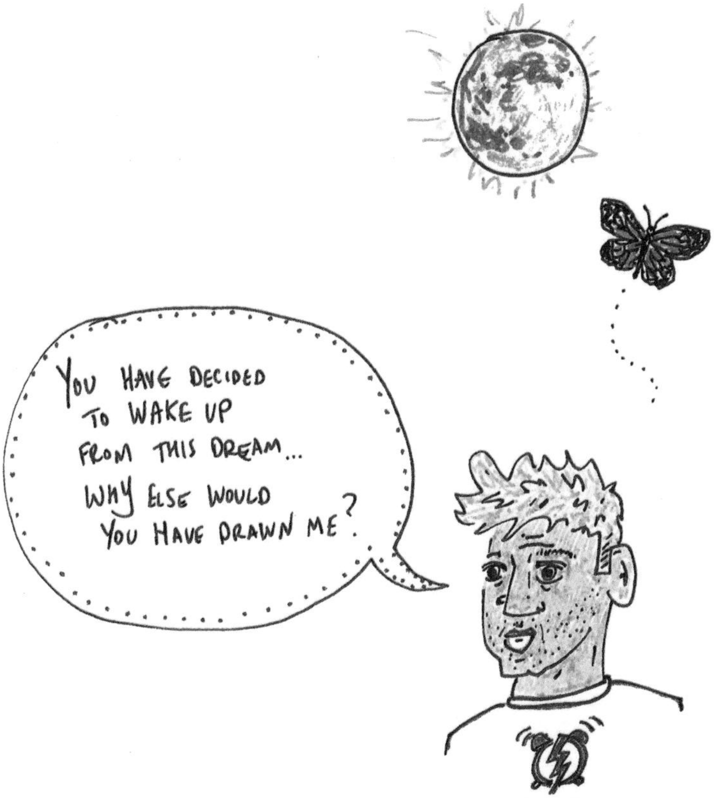
YOU HAVE DECIDED TO WAKE UP FROM THIS DREAM... WHY ELSE WOULD YOU HAVE DRAWN ME?

If we are the writer, producer, actor, director and audience, Then anything we draw, say & create is for "us." There's just one DREAM That we are all co-creating each moment. By writing These words, "I've" awakened another part of "myself." There are too many synchronicities and MAGIC moments to be a matter of chance. It's a personalized message written in The stars to call you back anew. The messages sometimes take multiple clues across years - but as you become aware of "WHO" is talking, you tune in. You can live your life closer to a waking dream - moving from intention to creation faster and faster. Evolving up the spiral of spirit to the level of Universe creator and beyond. This illustrated wake-up call was predetermined. "You" had encoded the perfect signals + signs to continue nudging you to your Greatest Journey & Greatest Work!

✦ FULL JOY ✦

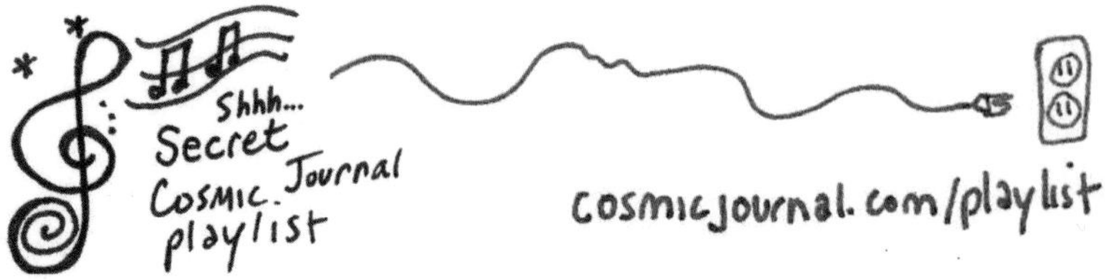
Shhh...
Secret
Cosmic Journal
playlist
cosmicjournal.com/playlist

You Are A Love Letter Written to... The Universe

The love you'll accept from others is to the same extent as the love you'll accept from yourself. My friend Kamal Ravikant wrote a book called "Love Yourself like your Life Depends On it." And it does. One exercise that seems so silly and so odd is to look at yourself in the mirror and keep saying

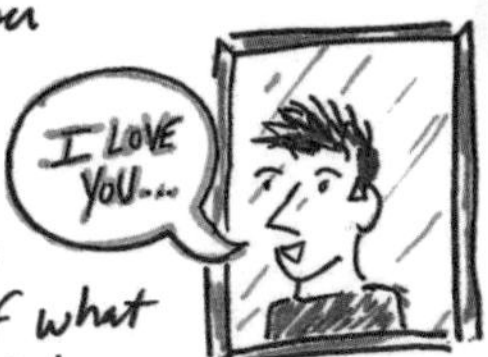
I LOVE YOU...

Look deep into your own eyes until you can actually see the Universe inside. Kamal had me do it for 5 min. and by the end you've changed... you've softened... you're connected to your higher self. To me, so much of what are seen as big issues can be solved by amplifying our own self-love and wholeness. Then we do not have the need to overpower someone else, to be bothered by those of different races, religions, etc. You don't need to numb yourself with alcohol or drugs. You wouldn't have to indulge in gossiping or even judging because you are content in your own skin.

[Loving yourself means loving yourself as an imperfectly perfect being - Forgiving yourself for the past and allowing yourself to BE.]

Loving yourself shows up in how you treat yourself. There cannot be guilt around ensuring you are whole. If your cup isn't full, you cannot pour into anyone else in your life. You don't need to sacrifice yourself.

Loving yourself is about nourishing your body, mind + soul. Taking time for meditation, yoga, recreation, play, adventures, connecting to what your heart calls for - and simply treating yourself in a loving, kind way. Being aware of what you tell yourself. Track your own dialogue - is it loving and supportive? Or do you constantly tell yourself to give it up, things won't work or discounting your aspirations? If you really, really love someone, you treat them differently than how most of us treat ourselves. Sometimes we treat our pets or even car better than ourselves. Love yourself fully + completely. Everything. YES Everything without judging... without complaining... without explaining. Love each little bit of your body, your talents, your ideas, your stumbles and your goofs. (yes, even the parts you believe couldn't possibly be lovable. They ARE.)

If you only knew a fraction of your luminance, you'd fall madly + totally in LOVE!

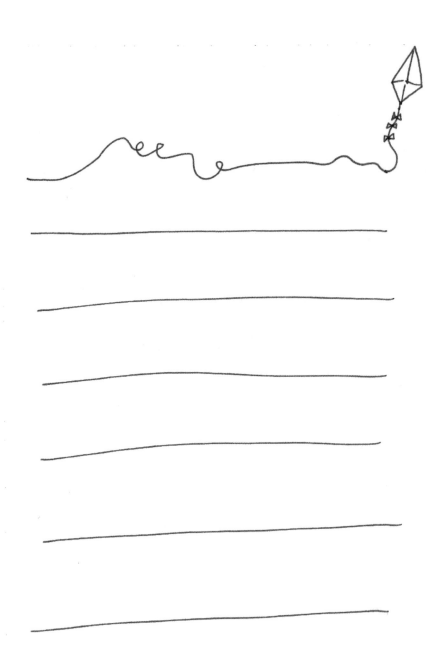

Don't hit SNOOZE -ON YOUR- COSMIC ALARM CLOCK

Everyone's COSMIC ALARM clock goes off at different times. It starts as a whisper, a small voice that gets louder + LOUDER until you either answer it or ignore it. For me, it was a simple question,

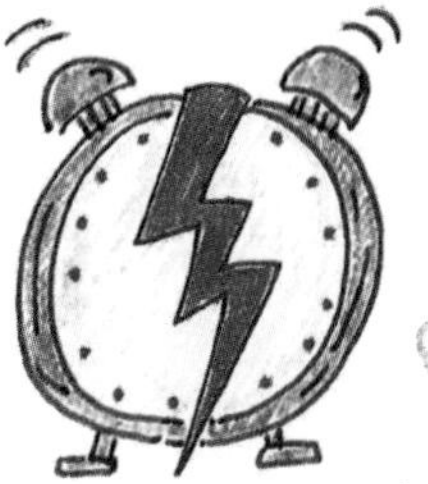

My daughter Zoe really wanted to lose her first tooth. She couldn't wait for her own "wiggly tooth" like her older brother. But you can't rush it. Like everything, There's a right time in the natural cycle...

"AM I HAPPY? AND WOULD I BE HAPPY 10 YEARS FROM NOW IF NOTHING CHANGED?"

Pretty simple question really - but if I was honest the answer was **NO!** From the outside looking in, Things should have been GREAT. I was making very good money while helping a lot of people. I had a good reputation in my space, great family, hot Sports car, etc. BUT deep down, I knew There was Something MORE. A greater way of putting all my talents, resources, network, expertise, AND full self into what's NEXT. I took a leap That turned into a "Bonk on the head." $400k

At That point I had 2 choices:

Back to my safe world and my "golden handcuffs"

OR

DOOR #2 Keep exploring & following my heart into The unknown.

You never quite know where you'll end up by answering your COSMIC ALARM CLOCK but I guarantee it'll be Somewhere greater Than you could have planned... in a different MAGICAL way. What I Thought would make me "happy" has expanded WAY beyond what I could have even imagined after making That leap.

ALIGN

your HEAD, HEART & HIGHEST PURPOSE (and happy child)

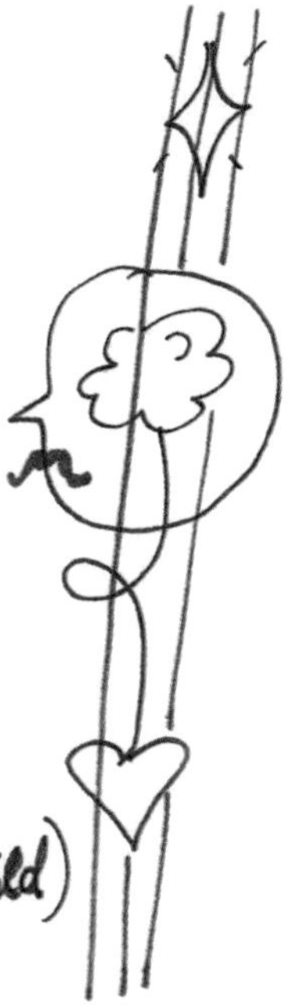

When you have full alignment, there's A massive
acceleration that happens. Like everything is Turbo-charged!
You are in <u>flow</u>. You are living your DHARMA.
You are "<u>lucky</u>!" Things "fall" into place for you.
It's too easy to live from our heads and over think
everything - but <u>our heart</u> is the real guide to where
we are headed because it connects to the <u>language without words</u>.
Our heart is what moves us closer + closer. to our
special + unique mission here in alignment with the Universe.
But you cannot just forget your head either, that's needed
for conceptualizing and Thinking as we move ahead. There's a
reason YOGA is so concerned with alignment. ~~The flow of~~
information up + down is unkinked. {You light up all the
way from top to bottom}

But don't get so serious as you
link up to your highest purpose. The most
spiritual people are some of the biggest
pranksters + professional laughers.
After all, it's all a BIG COSMIC Joke
anyway, and now you see the
punchline...

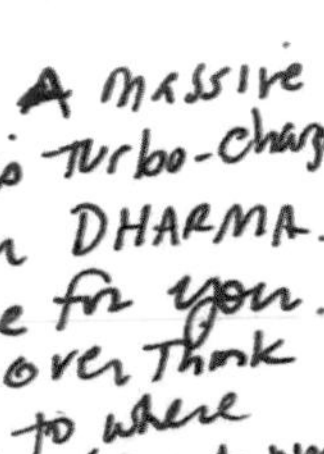

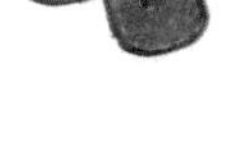

(Tickle your higher self for another clue to the joke)

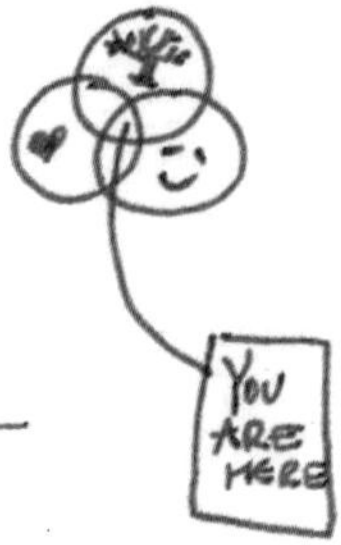
YOU ARE HERE

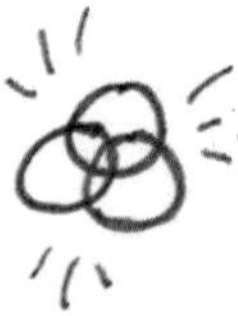

You Cannot Have Within You A TRUE DREAM Without Also Having the Way

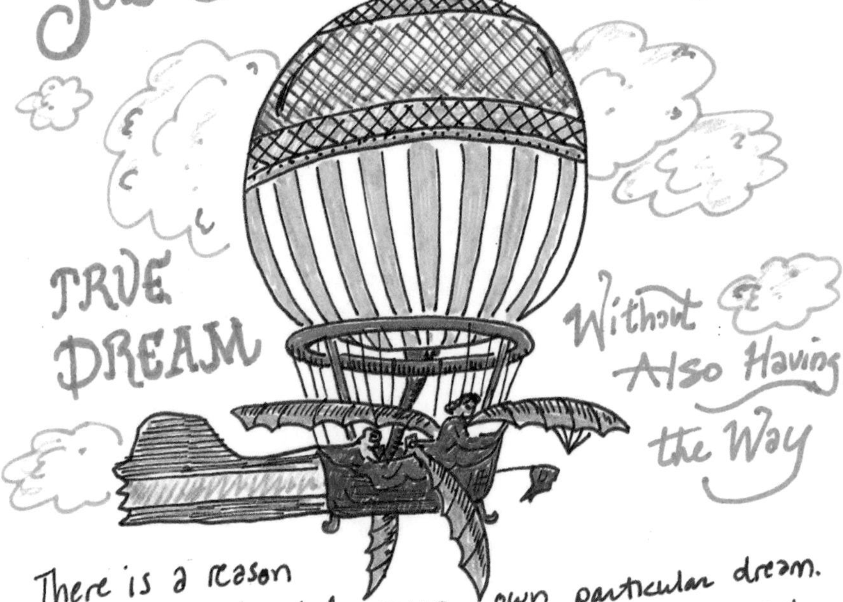

There is a reason you've been handed your own particular dream. The Universe wants to co-conspire with you to make it happen. If you have that kind of deep, deep burning desire, no dream is impossible. Hidden allies, forces and resources will move to open up new path-ways. If you look deep within your center and this dream speaks to your heart, it's for you - and you're for it. The way may not always be easy or even known, but as you travel down the first few steps, the next steps will open up. That's where MAGIC * happens - and your greatest growth. And if that dream is in service of the whole - even more doors open! You don't have to know how the dream will become real - You just need to trust it is sacred to you & others will join.

"What You Seek is ALSO Seeking You"

- RUMI

TAKE This journal to water...
a creek, pond, lake, river... the ocean.
Sit there and see how water would
answer your question here.

DO YOU WANT TO JUST PUSH MORE WATER DOWN THE RIVER

~OR~

DO YOU WANT TO CHANGE THE FLOW OF THE RIVER?

— ERIN PAVLINA

The same thing that got you where you are now won't get you to the next destination on your journey. The only way to grow is to continually express your deepest essence of your greatest gift.

It's too easy to just "push" more water down the river by simply doing what is easy and has worked for you before. For those of us who have accomplished "success," this is harder to really get behind...

I know this might seem a little strange, but have you ever felt like you are <u>DESTINED for Greatness</u>?

No, not in an egotistical way — but simply in a quiet, knowing way that you have been tapped to contribute something more. I've also heard that quiet voice in my ear, whispering about not fully living up to my vast potential. Pushing more water is about living someone else's dream for you. The way its always been done, dictated by your parents, society, tradition, etc. Your true path creates a new River of your choosing. It's your active choice — not a decision by default. It takes courage. Faith. Full alignment of your dharma. Your TRUTH.

धर्म

" It is better to fail at your own dharma than to succeed at the dharma of someone else. "
~ Bhagavad Gita

What's stopping you from doing exactly what you Thought of when you read This entry?
(Be honest)

_____

_____

_____

_____

_____

You sure it's TRUE?

_____

_____

_____

Following Your Heart
is Frequently Scary...
But Never Wrong

The Universe conspires with you to support you once you finally "jump." Only the times when you step to the edge and hesitate is there confusion. Your heart leads you to the path less taken. The path of trusting your inner guidance to nudge you to keep showing up in full service. For some reason, each time we follow heart, it seems scary until you realize you are fully supported every single time.

- ♡ -

I cannot recall one single time, with an elevated view, that I was ever upset I followed my heart. You cannot be mistaken in service of your built-in GPS. There is a certain strange PULL and allurement that simply will not quit. Your heart is that bridge between your cosmic blueprint and the perfect unfolding here. Now.

Q: What are you standing on the precipice of? Go ahead...

3... 2... 1...

♡ JUMP ♡
♡

23

TEXT·A·FRIEND
ROULETTE

Send This entry to a
friend and see what happens.
Or tell Them you were inspired
to Send This to Them as an answer
to Something They are working on.

Bonus: Try someone you haven't seen in 6 months

_____

_____

_____

_____

_____

_____

_____

_____

PHOENIX Rising

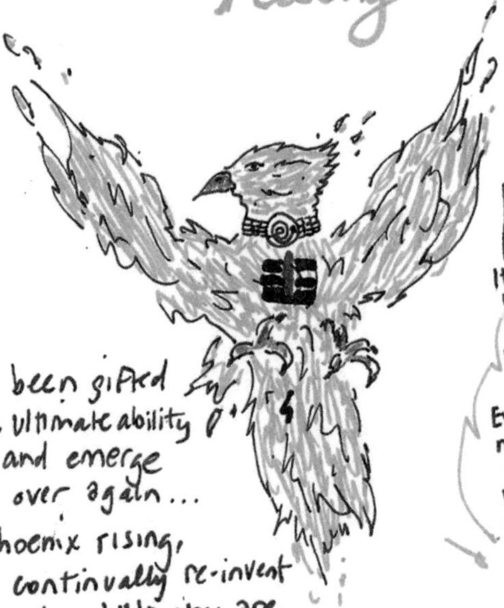

It's NOT about STARTING OVER

It's taking everything you've developed, succeeded with, "failed" at, struggled through and overcome.
Every relationship, network connection, good will cultivated, reputation built, skills and talent... everything is Now your new starting point

We have been gifted with the ultimate ability to arise and emerge over and over again...
Like a Phoenix rising, you can continually re-invent and remember WHO you are after the fires of purification burn down. The mythology of the fire bird is in our collective to provide the blueprint for your next breakthrough. The power of creative destruction to re-imagine fully without being tied to the past. This is even built into nature as some seeds actually are fertilized after a fire razes the land.

Are you ready to surrender your former smallness to your Destiny of Greatness? To fully step forward into the total transformation of your business, your life and your legacy... knowing you wont be the same again?
It's scary because our identities are so closely aligned to WHO we think we are with our existing world or previous accomplishments. But all of that is just "R&D" for what lies ahead... it's all brought you right here and right now to this moment.
Like a PHOENIX rising, your emergence into Joyful abundance is...
... INEVITABLE

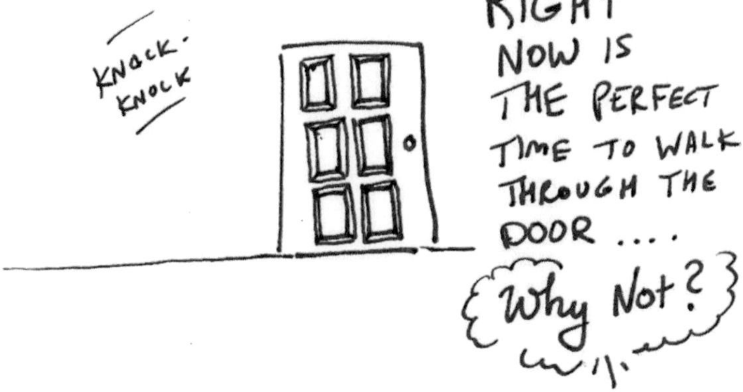
KNOCK-KNOCK
RIGHT NOW IS THE PERFECT TIME TO WALK THROUGH THE DOOR ....
Why Not?

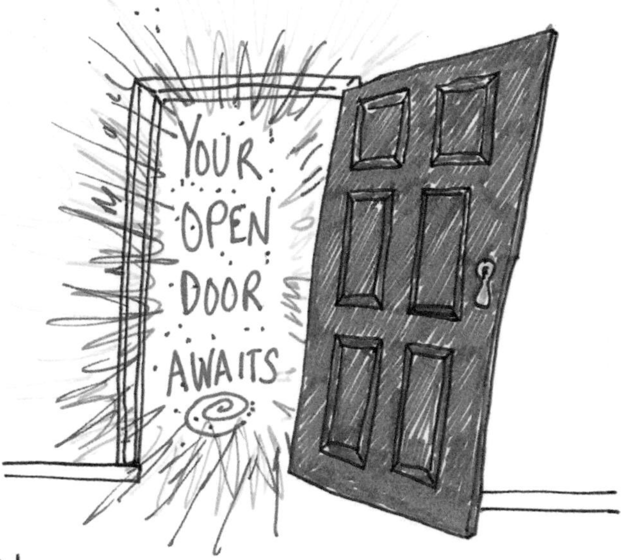
YOUR
OPEN
DOOR
AWAITS

You are always just one decision away from walking through the open door of your divine destiny. Sometimes you cannot see it is a door, but it's always there... awaiting you. The door is only locked if you think it is. Of course, you may not want to walk through. It might mean changing your friends, your habits, your identity & your place here. There's no lock on the door. No ogre or guardian... The limit is only how much you are willing to step fully to the other side. Realizing things will never be the same again. You cannot 'undo' this particular decision, which is why so many choose to knock or shuffle around the entrance hoping for a peek. That's not the way it works. You surrender fully and let go of fear... drop the stories holding you back from truly knowing what's on the other side.

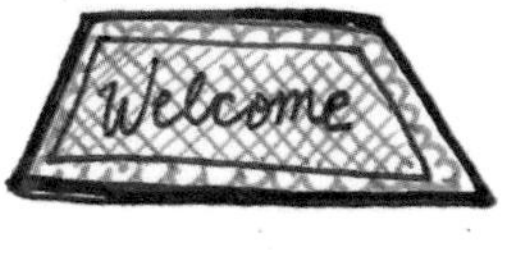
Welcome

_____

_____

_____

_____

_____

_____

_____

_____

_____

_____

RE REMEMBER

Your deepest Re·remembrance is not on a material level, it's on a deep spiritual level...

An intuitive perfection that you don't need to explain or put logic behind. (In fact, you probably couldn't fully.) You can feel it in a deeper part of yourself. A full knowing like awakening from a dream and seeing again. You are coming back to your center. Your origin point. There's nothing to learn or study, it feels like a perfectly worn pair of shoes you slip on or tailored suit. The knowing was designed for you by simply following your deepest callings and interests, no matter how odd or unsure you are.

In business you can cannot plan for it, but you can capitalize on it when it hits... if you have the courage to ACT. The flow of life has even more awaiting for you at every turn.

You're a multi-faceted bridge for extraordinary other you's at the highest level. They want your full and most beautiful expression of your true soul — not regular teachings.

Allow the fear of not making "enough" (impact, revenue, progress, etc) to be felt—but not given in to. By holding back your true artistry and full effort you can continue dreaming about potential instead of realizing it... NOW... Here...

There's nothing else to do. Effortless Effort.

RE·REMEMBER
YOUR PLACE AT
THE GALACTIC COUNCIL
AND YOUR CHOSEN MISSION HERE

29

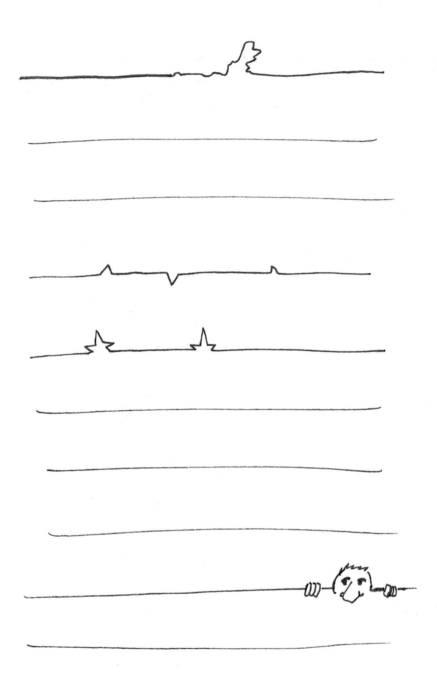

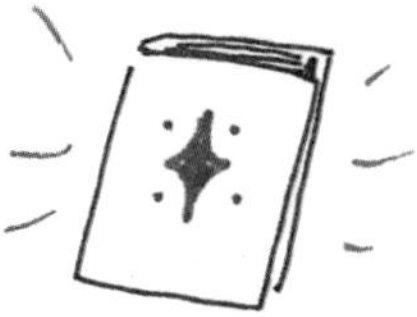

Journaling is your Journey home...

To some people a journal is just a blank book - but it's your *magical* tool. Peer reviewed scientific studies have shown journaling actually makes us happier. You just need to commit 10-15 minutes/day. Make it the same time each day and simply write. Journaling forces us to create a begining/middle/end for all those thoughts tumbling around in our heads. Put it in your journal + put it in writing. Typing isn't the same.

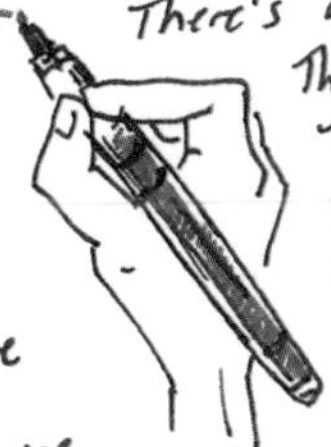

There's a deeper connection that happens when you write. If our journal is our magical place for exploring, doodling, dreaming and jotting down everything - then our pen is our *MAGIC wand!*

Allow yourself to pen your own future

What do I journal about?

- What's going on
- How you're feeling
- What you're grateful for
- Answers to Questions *
- Ideas
- Inspiring quotes + notes
- MAGIC you observe
- What gets you excited!

*Your Questions Create your Answers

Q: What would I do even if I failed?

Q: Who else has even more to gain by this succeeding?

Q: Am I Happy? And would I be Happy doing this 10 yrs from now?

Have fun with your journal + don't take it so damn seriously either. I let my kids draw in mine, and I love flipping through the pages, finding little "easter eggs" they've left me or even little notes + drawings I've done pages + pages ahead.

Ylusaba
(place of little fear)

-Wa·ak·ak·ak

WELCOME HOME

Klipfisant

If you listen closely, everything is sending you a message.... This morning one bird welcomed me home to wake me from meditation.

That's the thought... the word appeared as a feeling "HOME"

The concept of feeling at home. Being at home in our bodies, in our present situation, in our integrity, our alignment and presence. Home is safety + comfort. Safe that the Universe looks after you. Comfort in WHO you are... The perfect expression of infinite source.

When we arrive each time on Necker Island, the staff say, "Welcome Home." That's how burners greet each other too at Burning Man. Home is also where your "family" is. Your star family — we've reassembled and gathered together. Filling your own 'light circle' is part of coming home. The people who you immediately recognize; They share your heart. It's not something you can think into — only feel through the heart. Our heart is our beacon home to the stars.

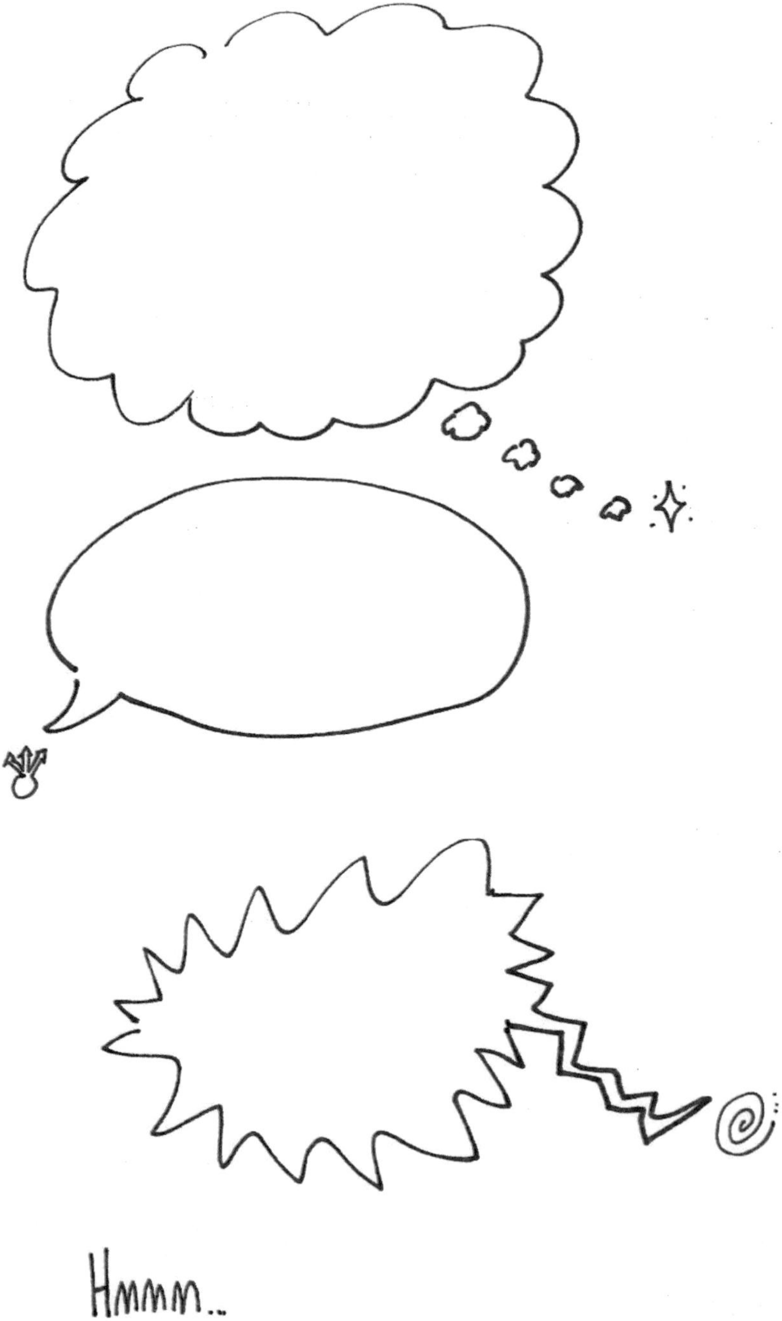

Hmmm...

WHY BLEND IN, IF YOU WERE MADE TO ~~STAND~~ OUT

P.S. Somehow we think we're being humble if we don't proclaim our greatness. To fully stand up and **BE** in our unique contribution...

The thing you do better than just about anyone else. Usually it is a combination of several talents and interests from your background. Nobody likes the overconfident boaster – but more times than not, we underestimate how valuable what we do really is. Sometimes it's because it comes so easy to us. But genius is in the combination of multiple areas that are perfectly natural for us! (And only you!) Stand fully in that perfect space. Deliver your greatest gift to the world! We're waiting...

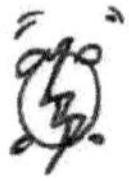

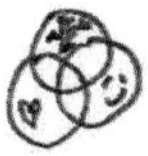

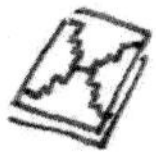

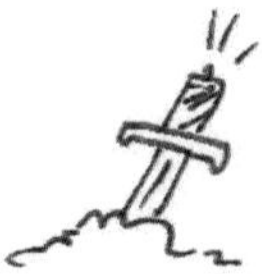

No matter how hard you struggle or "fail," you can always track your TRUE purpose by

JOY

Joy IS YOUR SOUL'S GPS

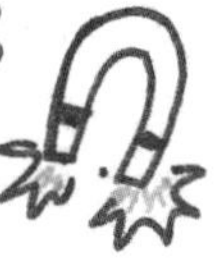

Such a subtle energy of truly feeling Joy. It's not happiness, that's fleeting. It's about feeling fully utilized. All your gifts, talents, past learnings, "wins" and "misses." EVERYTHING - but it comes as effortless effort. Even when things seem like they are going in the wrong direction, tap into Joy to get back on track. That's the language of your full heart. ♥ Joy provides energy. You channel INSPIRATION. Even the word itself holds an idea of what happens. In Spire means to breathe into - typically of a divine nature. Where does your inspiration come from? From your HIGHER purpose calling to you from beyond. The idea comes totally filled with energy to get it done! That's inspiration at work. It's part of your *COSMIC* download. Then enthusiasm takes hold. Again the words hold clues: Enthusiasm ... even saying the word leads to feeling enthusiastic! "be inspired or possessed by god."

WORDS create WORLDS

There's a reason certain ideas or things inspire us + the journey of Joy energizes us. This natural attractor is like a magnet if you let your heart + higher purpose guide you. A good question to ask is, "Is There Joy Today?"

You can only download what is in resonance with your frequency... Charged with Love & GRATITUDE + focused Meditation to see your TRUE PATH

DOWNLOAD

INSPIRATION

RETURN

"REAL"

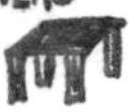

ENTHUSIASM

ACTION

DRAW + DREAM + DOODLE

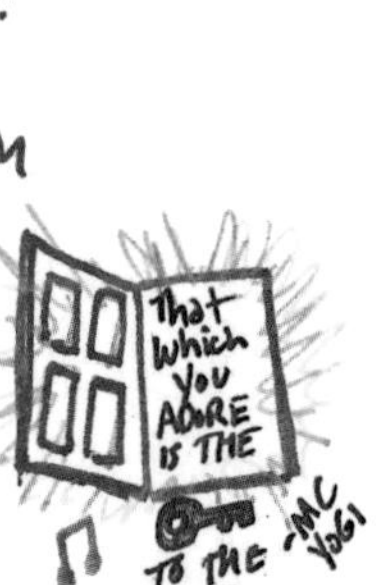
That which you ADORE is THE
TO THE DOOR
-MC Yogi

Pick a picture*
in your phone
That matches
the feeling
from This entry

What's the connection?

_____
_____
_____
_____
_____
_____

* Or look at the time right now and find
the picture That matches the hour, e.g. 12:08
Would be the 12th picture You took or go
back 12 pictures from today. Your choice.

Don't Regurgitate Rainbows

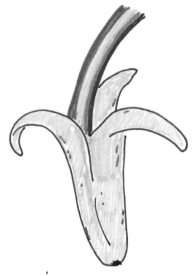

It's easy to simply parrot positive thinking and make everything a repeat of what your favorite guru said. You need your own take, view and filter instead of just being another voice saying nothing.

[Being your own voice means going further into your own true heart. Your true source. Uncover the deepest essence of You!]

What are the true teachings you have learned directly? Go to the edge and be the guide. Together we will explore boundaries with your fellow co-creators, instigators and catalysts. Your path is not just walking in the same footsteps of others before you, but also going further by lighting the way. You make your road by walking it.
(And then teaching it) ←
in your way

MEDITATION for SUPER, CRAZY-BUSY ENTREPRENEURS

A couple years ago, I would have laughed at the idea of Meditating. Yes, I knew there were lots of reasons to do it. I had heard lots of people share their stories and read scientific evidence on how meditation actually improves brain connections & health. It didn't matter, I still thought I had a million ideas a minute running around in my head and couldn't slow down.

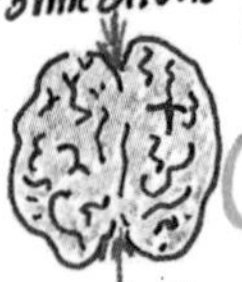

Q&A

Q: How long?

A: Even a few minutes works. It's better to meditate regularly than only a few times for longer periods

Q: What if I have a BIG idea?

A: Don't stop! Let it go. It'll come back... Or maybe not. Practice nonattachment.

Q: How long before I'm enlightened?

A: Now. Or maybe later.

One of my buddies, Vishen Lakihiani, puts on a personal transformation event called A-Fest (Awesomeness Fest). I was a speaker there and sat in on some of the other sessions including listening to Vishen talk about meditating (again!).

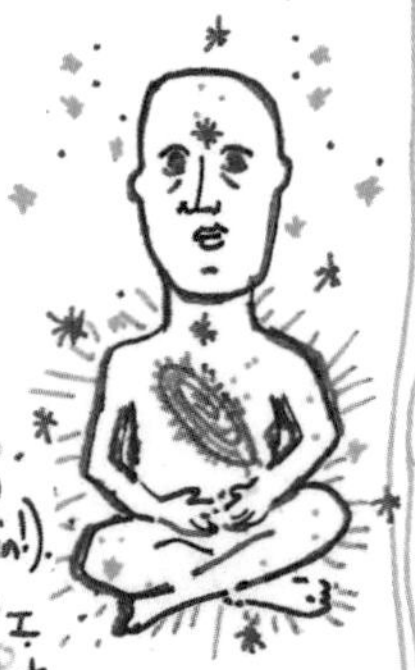

Since we were in Maui, I was inspired to try it while snorkeling so I could hear my breath.

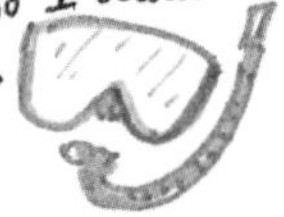

That worked - but never totally stuck...

Then I got a chance to interview the hip-hop mogul Russell Simmons. He's a huge advocate for meditation + yoga. I figured if this super high-energy entrepreneur could do it, I could too! For one week before I met with Russell, I meditated for 10-20 minutes per day using his mantra in his book Success Through Stillness. I like experiments, so I made this small commitment to myself to meditate at least 1X/day, just to see what happened. That was 5 years ago - and still going...

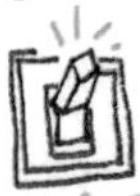

It's Not A light switch. It's a practice

I'm certainly not an expert, but I know it works.

- There is No wrong way
- Sometimes I meditate and still have all sorts of thoughts. It's OKAY. I return and focus on my breath.
- You can think of your thoughts like clouds that pass along the sky. Observe but don't judge.

Stillness leads to greater awareness, increased intuition and widening GAP Between STIMULUS & RESPONSE

"In that space is our power to choose our response. In our response lies our growth and our freedom."
- Viktor Frankl

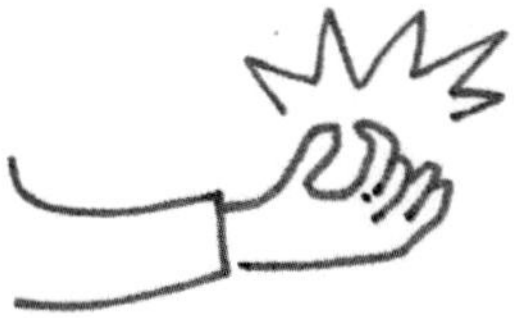

MEDITATE for 8 Minutes

Now What?

IN STILLNESS YOU MEET YOUR TRUE & SECRET SELF

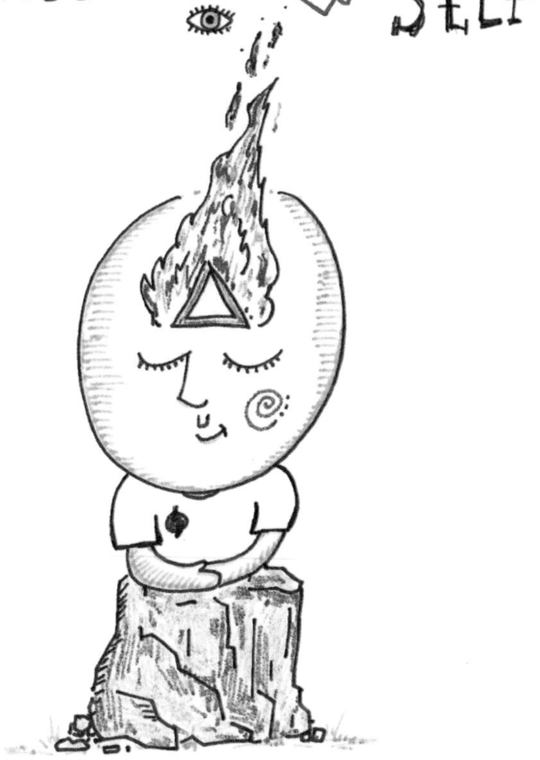

The World is noisy and always blinking, bleeping + vying for our attention. Stillness is a rare moment to shut out the other voices and hear with another set of ears. To see with expanded vision of what's really True. Quiet contemplation, meditation, mindfulness... or even doing "nothing"!.. all have great benefit to our always-on lives. When we pause fully, the ripples across the water of our minds can calm down so the Universe can converse with us. It's Subtle. It's a whisper. But everything is "talking" if we slow down to listen... awaiting the verse we will sing back to the greatest symphony. Our part in the mosaic of meaning woven through inspiration of the divine spoken in silence. Shhhhh...

Why?*

Why does this page matter to you right now?

(Whatever you answer, keep asking WHY to get deeper and deeper to the real WHY.)

ANSWER #1: _____

_____

_____

Why? _____

_____

_____

Why? _____

_____

_____

Why? _____

_____

_____

Why? _____

_____

_____

Why? _____

_____

Books Stack Your Positive Future

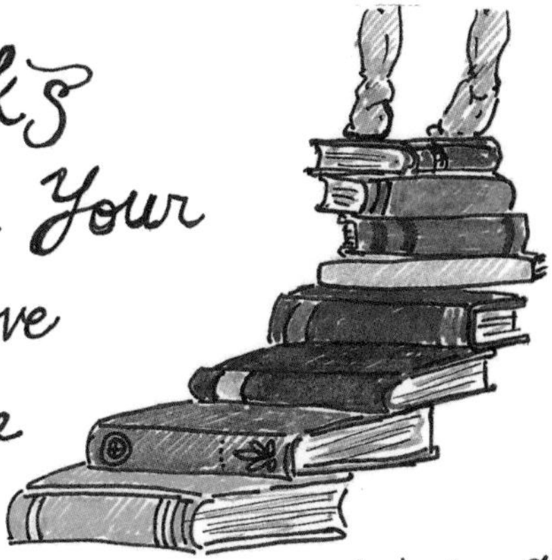

I believe your life changes from the books you read, the people you meet and the experiences you have. But to me, books are one of my greatest catalysts for thinking differently. Imagine, someone putting 10, 15, 25+ years of their life's lessons into the pages of their book, and then this distilled wisdom is waiting for you Anytime.

— ♦♦♦ — ♦♦♦ —

One of my early "mentors" was Earl Nightingale. I somehow found a set of his tapes when I was 17 or 18 and inside I heard a lesson I never forgot; if you wanted to become an expert in any subject, simply read or study 1 hr/day for 3 years. And to become a world-class expert, it's 1 hr/day for 5 years. I took that to heart and wondered what would happen if you read for 2 or 3 hours each day for years and years. That's how I became an "overnight success" story, 10 years in the making.

— ♦♦♦ — ♦♦♦ —

Books are mentors in print. And you can continue going deeper and deeper into any subject by finding who influenced that author's thinking. I love going further + further back into foundation material. When I was learning marketing, I wouldn't be content with the most recent book, I got more insights by digging into material from the turn of the Century... 100+ years back. That's where so many of the secrets and magic lie hidden. It is really MAGIC how certain books will show up in your life at the exact right time... and in unusual ways.

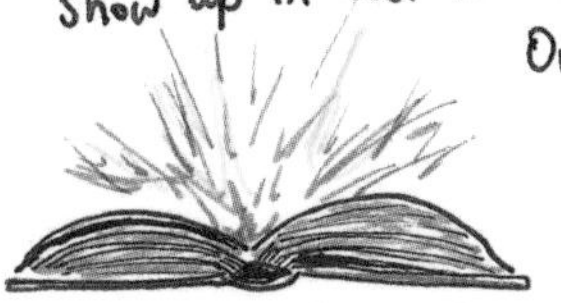

One night my wife, Missy caught a bug under the only heavy book by her bedside, and it turned into one of the most pivotal books I've read. Wow!

Here are a few that might be MAGIC for you too:

+ The Great Work of Your Life (Cope)
+ Living With Joy (Roman)
+ The Surrender Experiment (Singer)
  + The Untethered Soul
+ A Brief Tour of Higher Consciousness (Bentov)
+ Love Yourself Like Your Life Depends On It (Ravikant)
+ Daring Greatly (Brown)
+ Evolved Enterprise (Silver... yup me) :)

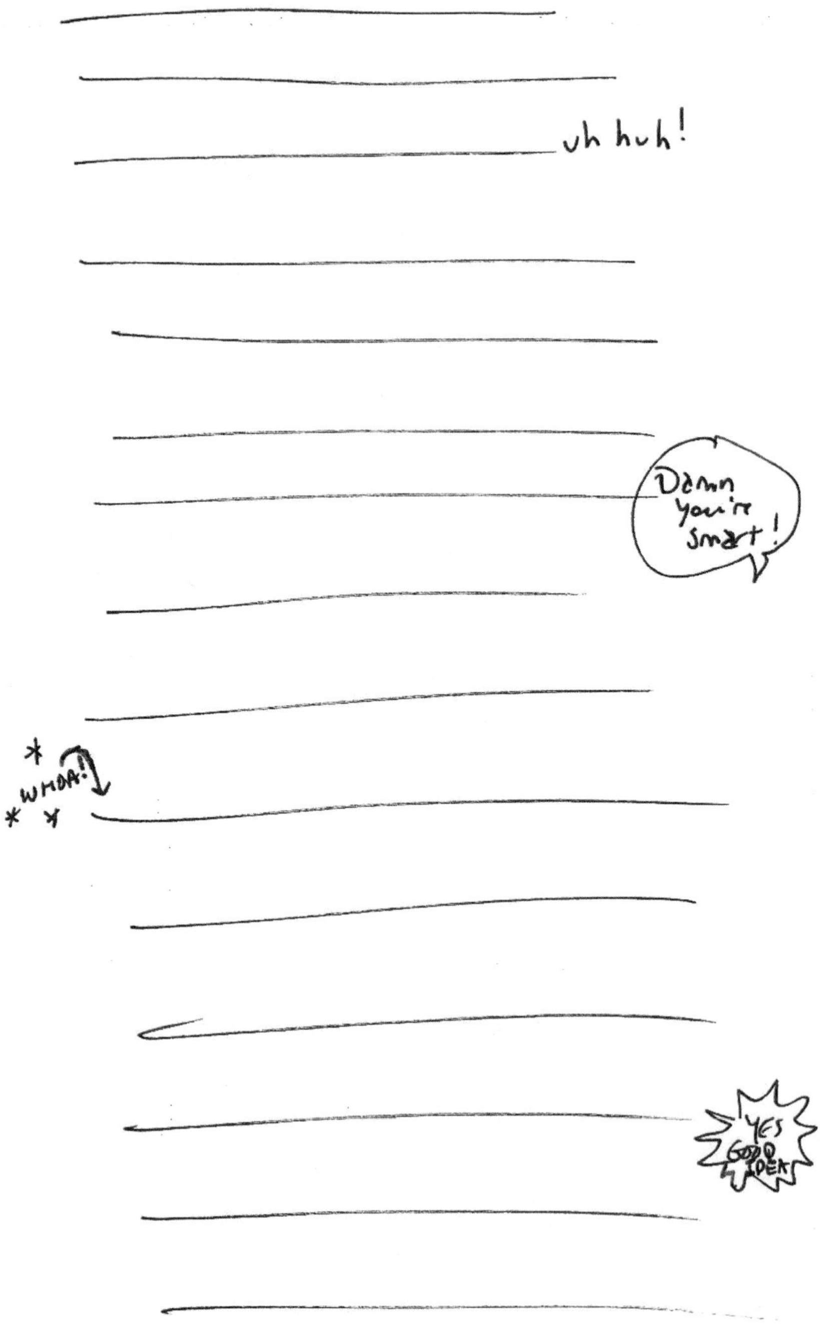
uh huh!
Damn you're smart!
WHOA!
YES GOOD IDEA

"YES"

What can you say ... to even more?

SAY YES TO:

* Fully Showing Up
* Playing More
* Resources + guidance
* Accepting help
* Amazing opportunities always opening
* My role in the greater COSMIC STORY
* Being in FULL ALIGNMENT
* Myself

Saying YES means being OPEN. Open to life. Open to new doors. Open to new ways for solving "problems." Problems are in quotes because so many times those "problems" are the right nudge or push to change directions... or find better opportunities.

SAYING YES IS ALLOWING

Allowing the flow of life to have your back! Why not add more YES into your world? One of our family's "SILVER KEYS" is the value of saying "YES" intentionally for one week. Teaching them to try new foods, new things and just being willing to meet life openly. I've always believed you regret more the things you didn't do than what you did do. So why not say YES to those opportunities before you even know for sure if they'll be defining moments in your life? But only those willing to say YES will know...

YES IS THE OPEN DOOR

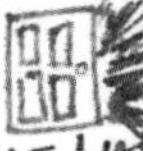

THAT WAS PREVIOUSLY CLOSED.

GIVE IT A TRY? HINT: SAY YES!

TRY THIS "YES EXPERIMENT"

1. WRITE THE WORD YES IN YOUR JOURNAL OR AHEAD IN YOUR CALENDAR ON RANDOM PAGES.
2. Any day it appears, be open to saying YES all day
3. Share what happened with your YES experiment

optional TAG #CosmicYesExperiment so we can find each other

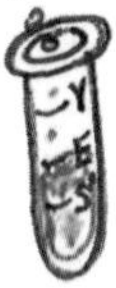
Y
E
S

Q: What would your 11-year-old self tell you about what you just read?

A: _____

_____

_____

_____

_____

_____

_____

_____

EXPLORE

YOU
LIGHT
THE WAY

You only see the way by making the way. Your
light grows brighter + brighter with a clear heart.
You've designed an epic journey awaiting you, leading
by following your heart. JOY is your trail marker.

As you light this path yourself, you automatically
forge the path forward for others. Simply by sharing,
experimenting and feeling your own way ahead,
the guideposts are put down. Not for others to
follow exactly in your footsteps but to be
empowered to find their own way... in the exact
pattern + sequence designed for them. And at the
'end' of the journey re-remembering your wholeness...
AGAIN & AGAIN.

TEXT-A-FRIEND ROULETTE

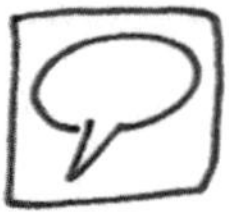

Send This entry to a friend and see what happens. Or tell Them you were inspired to send This to Them as an answer to something They are working on.

Bonus: Try someone you haven't seen in 6 months

THE UNIVERSE AMALGAMATED, LTD
DIVISION OF Vandelay Industries
33133
Sept. 25, 1973
PAY TO THE ORDER OF
YANIK SILVERSTARSEED
10,000,000.—
Ten Million 00/100
INFINITE DOLLARS
For: Catalyzing the Catalysts
1: 004200 1: 314159265359 11° 33133

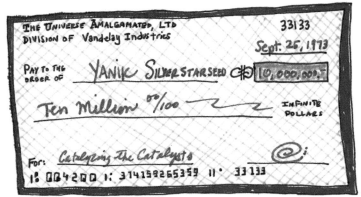

"What Would You Do If You Were Handed a $10 Million Check? What Would Stay The Same & What Would Change?"

— Eric Lochtefeld

That's one of my friend Eric's favorite questions for establishing a baseline for your bliss. One of the best indicators that you're doing what you are meant to is by separating out the finances. How many people, even entrepreneurs (who control their destiny), would still be doing what they're doing most of the day?

Ten Million is a number that I know several of my friends have thought about as financial security. That's the number I wrote in my journal many years back before my 40th as my ideal. When I hit that milestone, I found that entry and Missy asked me if I was upset I didn't hit that goal. I said, "No, because I got the essence." The intention was about working on what you want with who you want and when you want. I don't have that perfectly, but there is a whole lot more I'd keep when I'm handed that check. What I realized is it's about the feeling that number may give you....

= Joyful Abundance =

Multiple doors in all directions opening wide... but not just revenue. Everything!

Imagine, on the day you were born, the Universe set up an unlimited bank account drawn on INFINITE DOLLARS paid to you for rendering your unique contribution to evolution... Your ONE THING. This currency is better than dollars, euros or even bitcoin. Infinite rewards showing up for you when you do your assignment with your highest purpose for WHY you are here... right NOW.

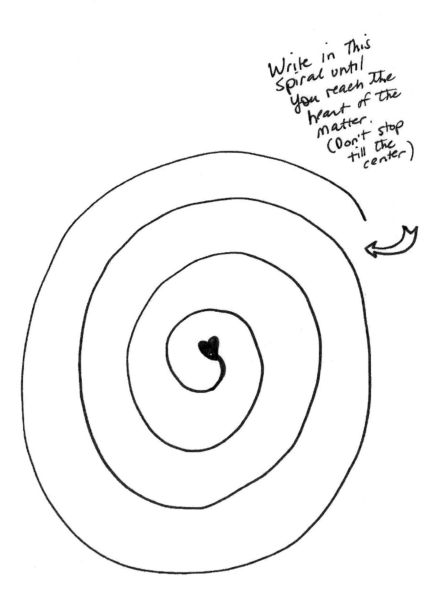

Write in This
Spiral until
you reach the
heart of the
matter.
(Don't stop
till the
center)

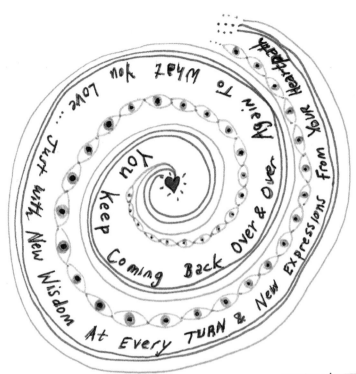

You

You Keep Coming Back Over & Over Again To What You Love ... Just With New Wisdom At Every TURN & New Expressions From Your Heartpath

What pulls at your heart has never been haphazard. It is preparation to continue refining your joyful expression. The essence never changes but the expression evolves with your knowledge and experiences - to see deeper ways to fully integrate what you love! As a kid I really loved drawing + art, I loved anything to do with sacred sites like the pyramids, and I was the class clown. Even this cosmic journal is an evolution of that heartpath. We keep coming back to things we love, or talents, but in new, more expanded ways. One of my friends loved promoting parties and producing the VIP experience, now he does it for leading entrepreneurs with greater purpose. One of our Maverick members was a leading investigative journalist but then retired — and now many years later she's sidelined her software company to create a hugely popular interview series of successful female founders. Anything you loved, especially as a kid, can be brought back into your life + business. Or particular talents you might have out-grown, but you can reapply them in new ways that have a greater capacity to help more people. There's a reason for each of the pieces of your history to pull together the perfect combination of GENIUS and brilliance that is YOU... and only YOU!

TWO

This world is seemingly designed on the concept of polarity and duality. To experience cold you need warmth. For hunger there is fullness. To be in a relationship shows us the contrast and reflection. Our light side also has a shadow side. These two aspects are intertwined in harmony, back and forth. The perfect paradox.

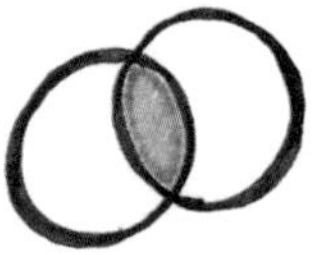

Male and female represent different aspects of our essence. Not just gender but energy. Push. Pull. Active. Receptive. The dance of universal forces. Finding that beautiful balance between the two sides.

Creating the balance of opposing forces in cooperation.

- Effortless Effort -

The narrative too many of us have been told is one side is right. One view is correct. One way to get where you want to. One side wants to blame the other in politics, in relationships, in agreements. Peace comes from bridging the polarity and seemingly opposite views + ideas.

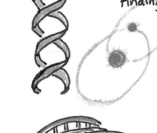

Left ⟷ Right
Modern ⟷ Ancient
Heart ⟷ Head
Commerce ⟷ Impact
Logic ⟷ Intuition
Spirit ⟷ Science
Receive ⟷ Give
MALE ⟷ Female
Attraction ⟷ Repulsion
LIGHT ⟷ Shadow

Two asks us to look in the mirror and see the "other" in ourselves. What attracts us and what repels us? What do we appreciate about the "other" and ourselves?

Everything is in CONNECTION — ONE to the OTHER.

What Story Are You Seeing?

You get to decide if something is "good" or "bad." "True" or "false." It's all in the meaning you give it. Also one person may experience the exact same set of facts or a situation and see things completely differently. Once we label it, then it takes on that story. Perhaps by flipping your view, you'll see things differently, like on this page...

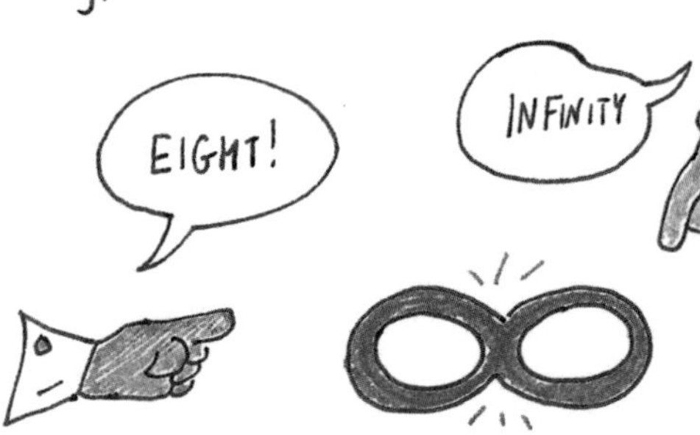
EIGHT!
INFINITY

I've always considered that everyone can justify their actions. Unless they're completely off, everything they do is "right" to them in light of the current situation. You can try truly looking at whatever is happening to you and see if you can play a game. You might believe it's "not good," but what could happen in the future to make it "good"? And in the same way. There's an old story of a Chinese farmer who had tended his fields for many years until one day his horse ran away. Hearing the news, his neighbors say this is "bad luck." The farmer replies, "Maybe." Then the horse returns with more wild horses. "Good luck!" Perhaps. As the farmer's son tried to tame the wild horses, he broke his leg. Again the neighbors extend their sympathy. "Such bad luck." The farmer is unfazed again, "Maybe." Then a conquering army is coming through the village to draft young men, and the farmer's son escapes being sent to battle because of his broken leg. The neighbors claim this is "good luck" but the farmer says, "maybe," again and so it continues

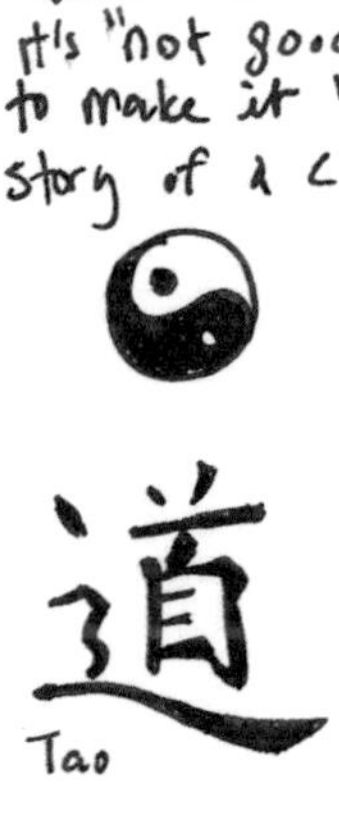
道
Tao

Your Destiny
is calling

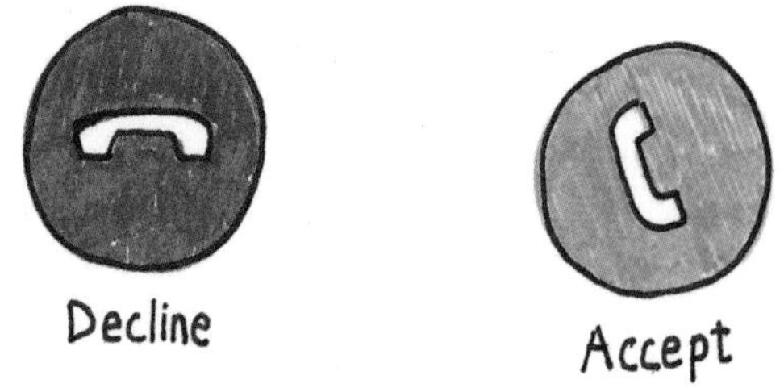
Decline
Accept

The Universe continues to send us signs, symbols, meetings, opportunities and challenges to nudge us to our Destiny unfolding. In each of these moments, we can choose to answer or let it go to voicemail.

Typically these "calls" come at, what we consider, less than perfect timing. It takes courage and faith to answer. Is it a spam robo call or a sacred call? So many of us want a better way or better business... we pray for help... but how many answer the call?

That call might not be a number you recognize... it might be a "random" area code or "butt dial." But (hee hee) just maybe... there are no accidents. The next person who calls you can be part of your BIG story.

(And no, texts don't count.)

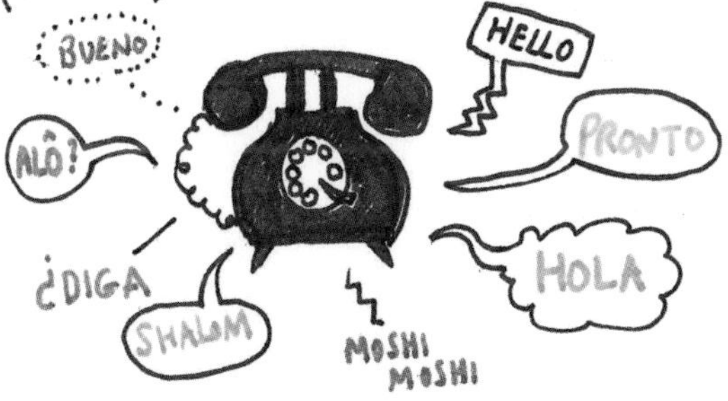
BUENO
HELLO
ALÔ?
PRONTO
¿DIGA
HOLA
SHALOM
MOSHI MOSHI

"YES AND"... NOT BUT

YES AND _____

_____

_____

YES AND _____

_____

_____

_____

YES AND _____

_____

_____

_____

_____

"And Wait, There's More..."

I love the notion of the ampersand and what it
brings together —
   "And wait, there's more"...
   "Yes, and..."
   "This and That"...
   "Rock and Roll"
AND is about including - not closing off options. Think
about pairing unlikely combinations, peanut butter + chocolate
Unlikely partners, Patagonia joined with WAL-MART to create
a coalition of apparel manufacturers + sellers to exchange notes,
best practices + help save resources. Creativity is a BIG
part of mixing different ingredients and pieces together.
Look at Hamilton: Hip hop, musicals, rap, etc.

UNLIMITED
POSSIBILITY OPEN
OPPORTUNITIES
      + COMBINATIONS
      + JOINT VENTURE
      + CO-CREATION
      + PARTNERS
      + COLLABORATION
      + CONNECTIONS
      + COMMUNITIES
      + PAIRINGS

61

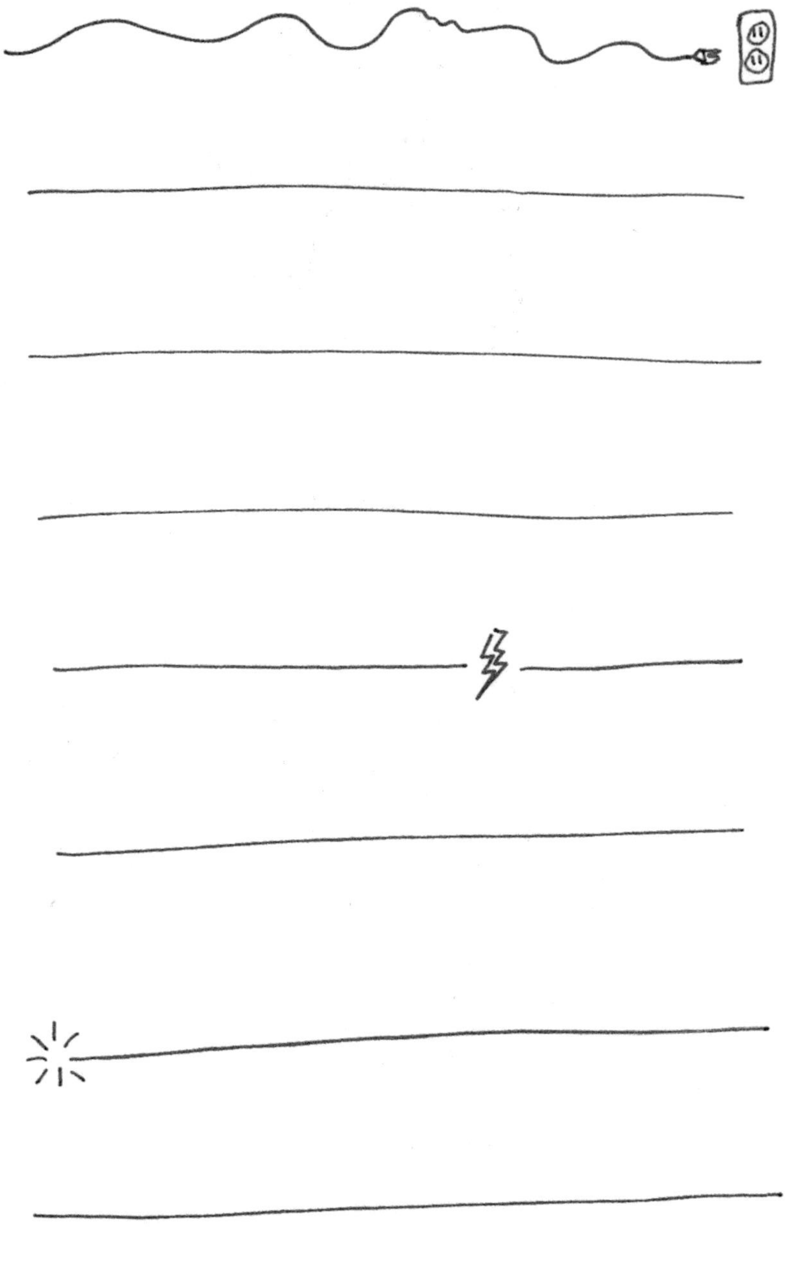

Why Not?

Too many of us talk ourselves out of whatever we really want because we don't think it's possible...

You've heard it before that if you don't ask- you don't get. You have to be in the "game" to play. We have our own internal "thermostat" for everything in our life. How easy or hard certain activities would be... our tolerance for TRUST and risk... our identity of our skillsets... what we think we can accomplish... what we need permission for... WHO we can meet... what others might do (or not do) for us... really .... ALMOST everything!

Sometimes you can borrow the belief you need from someone else you respect or look up to. I remember one friend would always find a spot at the crowded bar everytime we went out. He just knew he would. What if you simply hold the feeling of quiet, confident cheerful expectation? That it will work out perfectly... no matter what... but at the same time without expectation of how you want it. [Seems like a Paradox] Yes, your expectations are how events, people, and circumstances will come together (sometimes in the (IT IS) most MAGICAL way) for your best possible outcome. But you can't just expect whatever you want to show up at your front door. You meet in the middle - by starting and asking...

WHY not?

63

Why?

Why does this page matter to you right now?

(Whatever you answer, keep asking <u>WHY</u> to get deeper and deeper to the real WHY.)

ANSWER #1: _____

_____

_____

Why?

_____

_____

_____

Why?

_____

_____

_____

Why?

_____

_____

_____

Why?

_____

_____

_____

Why?

_____

_____

"I Don't Know" ...

It's absolutely + totally okay to say, "I don't know." Somehow we think we're supposed to have all the answers. I respect someone much more when they tell me these words... Today more than ever, the rate of exponential change means even what you thought you knew yesterday might not be the case. What's possible, what's "good" for you, how things are supposed to be, and maybe even what we believed as fact or "truth."

Why not be open to the unknown?

Embrace ambiguity to create Joyful Byproducts you never even considered.

Allow. The Great Mystery to unfold To simply know you can be at peace without knowing how this chapter will end*.. but absolutely knowing how the story ends. Full circle. Loving embrace with the DIVINE.

*or even this page... (I didn't)

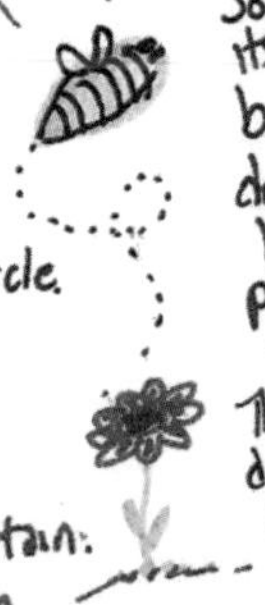

Sometimes its like the bee who doesn't even know she's pollinating the world. They're just drawn to what attracts them!

We want to know. We want to be certain: Sure we are going down the right path, making the right decisions, drawing the bee correctly. (Ha! or maybe that's just me.)

What if you're doing birthdays WRONG?

(I don't know)

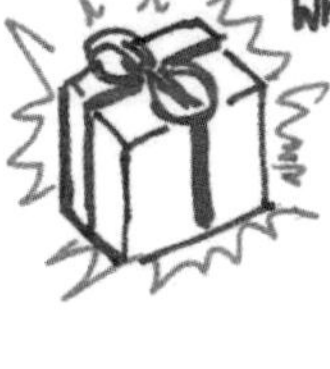

one country's traditions has the birthday boy or Girl giving presents to those people who impacted them most last year.

WHAT IF?

There Wasn't
A WRONG Decision?
A WRONG TURN?
A WRONG CHOICE?

What if all roads lead to the SAME PLACE of Perfection?

TEXT-A-FRIEND ROULETTE

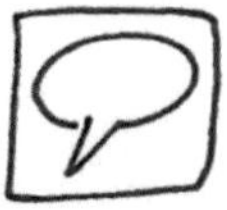

Send This entry to a friend and see what happens. Or tell Them you were inspired to send This to Them as an answer to someThing They are working on.

Bonus: Try someone you haven't seen in 6 months

EMBRACE
Fully

Ganesh is the remover and placer of obstacles. What if any ▨▨ "obstacle" you encountered was really there to steer you in the right direction you needed to go? How different would you look at them? Sometimes we are blocked and frustrated but realize how that was the best for us, ultimately. From an elevated view, all paths lead to the same place. Your return path to true re-remberance. Embrace fully each potential roadblock, obstacle, frustration or setback as a way to recalibrate towards your TRUE destination of destiny. And when you are in alignment and attuned to that place, allow Ganesh to then become the remover of obstacles. Say "YES" to it all! Fully embrace everything with wonder, awe, appreciation + grace to navigate the dream unfolding.

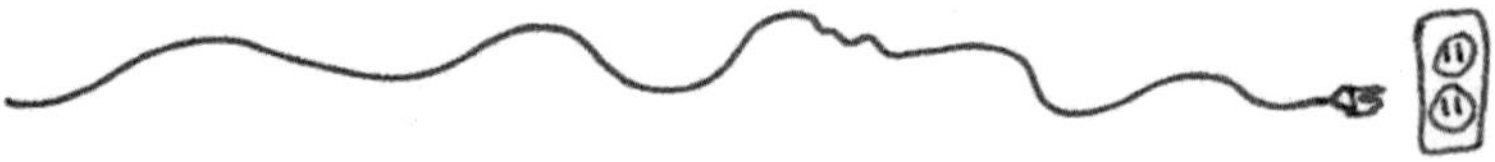

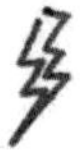

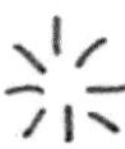

"There is a CRACK in Everything... that's how the light gets in."

-Leonard Cohen

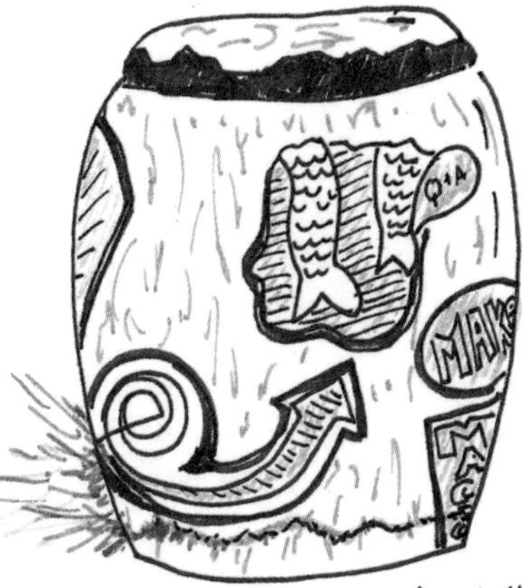
Q+A
MAKE

I received a beautiful, personalized "appreciation" jar from my friend, John Ruhlin. He is a master at gifting and flew in to personally hand deliver this beautiful piece of art customized for me. It spelled out M·A·V·E·R·I·C·K in pictures representing stories from my life like adventures, @↗ evolved enterprise, adventures, Q+A w/ Richard Branson wearing mermaid tails, my work in Haiti and more. Incredibly meaningful. I wrapped it carefully on the way home but perhaps not well enough. I put my bag down on the hard floor in the bathroom and I had a bad feeling, "Oh oh!" CRAP! Checking the bag I heard the distinct sound of pieces shaking. I was annoyed at myself for 30 seconds and then immediately thought of one of my favorite notions Leonard Cohen sings of in 'Anthem.' This crack is our humanness... being perfectly imperfect. More accurately it's the embracing of our shadow side as Jung describes it. The parts we'd rather hide. Or the "pain" we go through. To give in to it until we crack and then we grow. There's a gift there. A gift of greater empathy to others, a gift of resilience, a gift of being okay in all ways. All of these contain gifts we can take with us to the next stage of our path. I actually like my jar even more now. It has character. It has a greater story. The Japanese have a c cept called wabi-sabi, a view of finding beauty in imperfection. Appreciating the irregularity and authenticity that comes from the human artist. You cannot fake this kind of "perfection." Sometimes artists will deliberately create mistakes in their pieces to remind themselves of these concepts. Navajo Rug weavers would leave little imperfections called ch'ihónít'i – essentially "spirit line."

侘寂

wabi-sabi

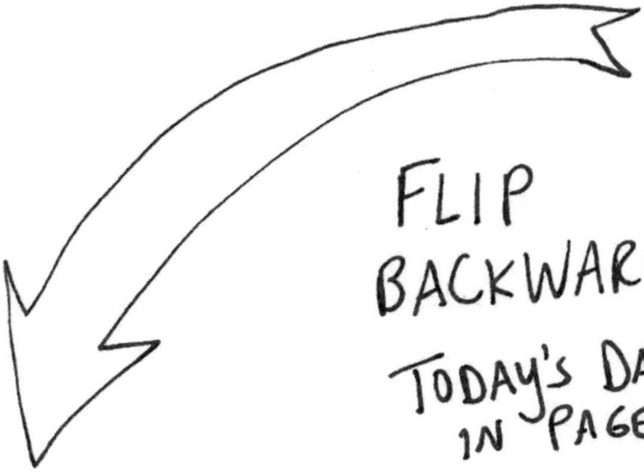

FLIP BACKWARDS

TODAY'S DATE IN PAGES

e.g. July 6
you flip
back 6 pages

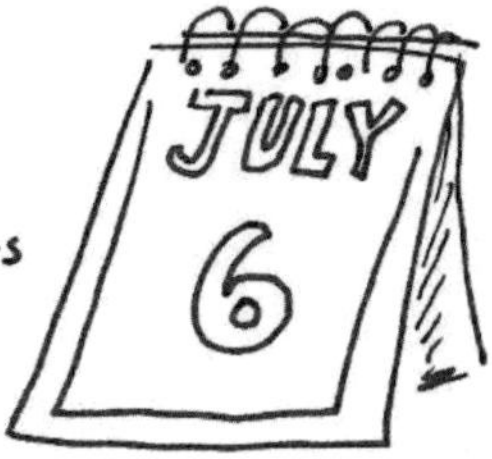
JULY
6

See ya on the flip side

How do these connect?

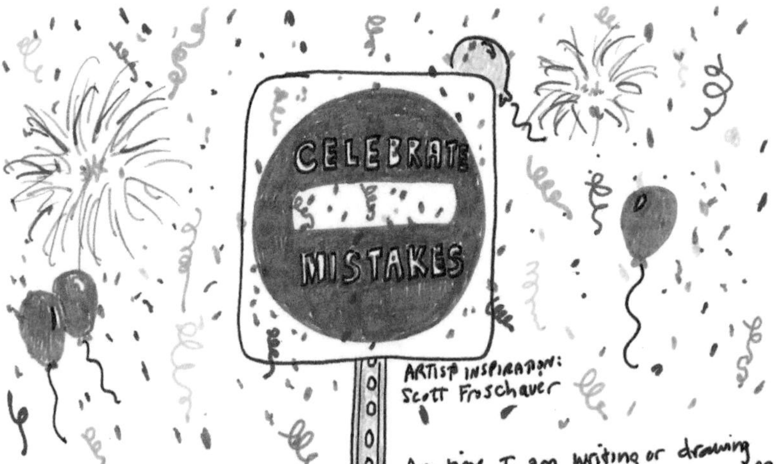
CELEBRATE
MISTAKES
ARTIST INSPIRATION:
Scott Froschauer

Sometimes the hardest part for an artist is making that first mark or brushstroke. Staring at the blank page or blank canvas is sometimes terrifying because of the fear of making a "mistake."

We are all artists of our lives so we need to remove that critic from our heads looking over our shoulders. You've heard that little voice...

"Is that going to work?"

"What if we look stupid?"

"Now, you screwed up!"

"You should have used pencil first."

"Did you spellcheck?"

"Oh oh - what if someone has a better version?"

"That doesnt even look like a ____."

"Is this really good enough to get out there?"

"Shouldn't I wait until I think about this more?"

"If you screw up this presentation - it'll really cost you..."

BLAH... BLAH... BLAH...

—ETC. ETC. ETC. ETC. ETC. —

Anytime I am writing or drawing or creating (in any way) I turn off that part of my analytical mind. I go back later and edit or think more through an idea - but you cannot create and critique at the same time.

Drawing has given me a new lens to look at "mistakes" - I see them as gifts. What else can I make them into? How else does it work better? One quote was totally mis-written and it turned out to have bigger implications than if I could have planned it that way. Mistakes need another name. We get scared to act or do because we are afraid of not succeeding or being perfect. What if mistakes were feedback? More like guardrails steering you towards your true path? When I interviewed selfmade billionaire Sara Blakely, she said her dad often asked her what she had failed at that day? If you weren't "failing," you weren't DOING. Frank McKinney, one of my mentors, would tell his daughter, Laura, that "C's" in school meant,

"SEE (C) I'M SMART"

Mistakes can be made into badges of honor because we keep learning + growing.

(P.S. Spot all my mistakes - not on purpose)

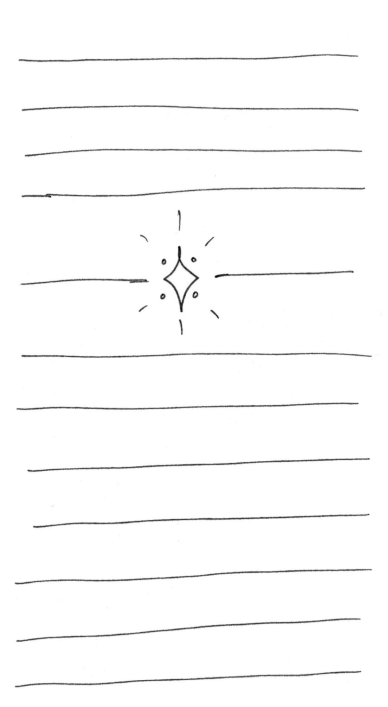

Inspiration: Sir John Tenniel, 1865

¿Quién eres?

(Ooh, wa, ooh wa,
Ooh, wa, ooh wa)
- The WHO

Who are you? (seems so easy, right?)
That's what the caterpillar asked Alice...

You are **NOT** your name, your ancestry, your job, your story, your body, your mind, your image, your bank account, your press clippings, your successes, your "failures," ~~your job~~ typos your family, your nation, your things, or your...

(THE More You Ask... THE DEEPER You GO)

YOU ARE

This is my list.
Write your own.

KEEP ASKING!

WHO???

- Father
- Husband
- Brother
- Son
- Entrepreneur
- Adventurer
- Catalyst
- Artist
- Light Bringer
- Everyone
- Storymaker
- Divine Destiny unfolding
- Galactic Seed blooming
- Perfect Oneness
- Everyone
- THIS

- Middleway
- Maker
- Bridge builder
- Architect of JOY
- Divine Spark
- Starseed
- An illusion
- Dreamer
- The actor, director & audience
- The forgiven
- You
- Pure peace
- The fruit
- Infinite Source
- Consciousness
- The Change Point

THE UNNAMEABLE
- ONE -

{THE ONES WE HAVE BEEN WAITING FOR}

A BEING OF SILVER VIOLET flame

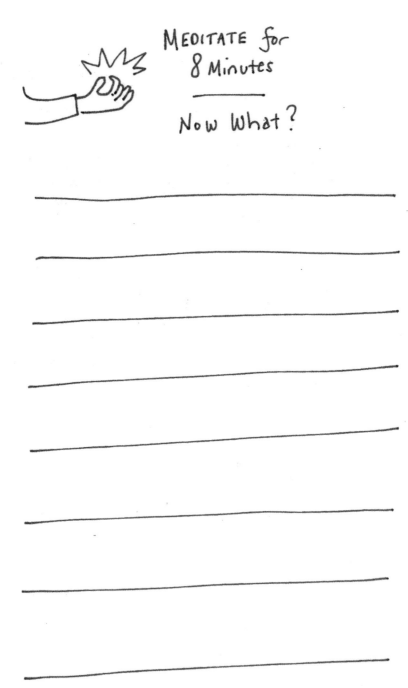

MEDITATE for
8 Minutes
_____

Now What?

YOUR QUESTIONS

CREATE YOUR ANSWERS...

I love questions. The better questions you ask, the more powerful the answers are. Some of the best questions can continue over many years actually. For whatever reason, we are designed to seek out answers to the questions we ask. You might wake up with an insight or even get an 'aha' while you're in the shower or taking a walk. But asking that poignant question sets you up for the beautiful answer

I like writing down a question on the top of a page in my journal and then writing multiple answers. Many times the first few answers are pretty pedestrian, but if you keep pushing yourself you'll get some real insights... even wilder answers. Don't censor yourself - just write. Also check out my friend Bill Dorius' material on intuitive writing & his book "Thought Revolution." After you're used your dominant hand to answer, you engage your non-dominant hand. I promise you'll be surprised by those answers.

Some of my favorite Questions:

Q: 10 years from now, will I be happy with what I'm doing?

Q: Who has even more to gain from this succeeding?

Q: What is the TRUE essence of what I want?

Q: What would I do even if I knew it would fail? (Brené Brown)

Q: What would my 111-year-old self tell me?

Q: If I knew the answer, what would it be?

TEXT ROULETTE

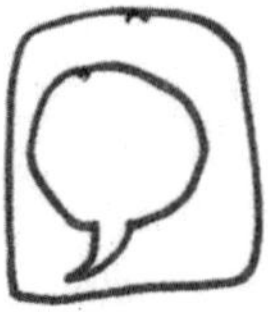

Ask a random contact to send you one letter of the alphabet. Then ask two more people to do the same until you have three letters. Now look at the entry and see the first three words that contain those letters:

letter ____________________

letter ____________________

letter ____________________

Now create a more empowering story for yourself using the three words above.

____

____

____

____

____

YOUR WORDS CREATE WORLDS

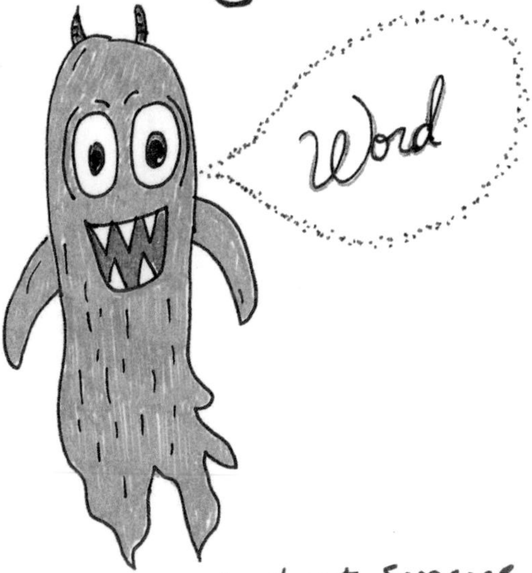
Word

You can learn so much about someone simply by paying attention to their words and language. What we say (or think) determines what we believe is possible or impossible. Phrases like, "I can't," or "I'll try," indicate they've given up before even starting. Stop yourself and slow down to really examine what you're telling yourself. Your words invoke what's "REAL." Take apart your next excuse and really observe what you're saying. Is it even true? Why are you repeating it? Where did it come from? What are the empowering words you could use instead? Words are alive with real power — ensure you are using MAGIC words to open up more worlds.

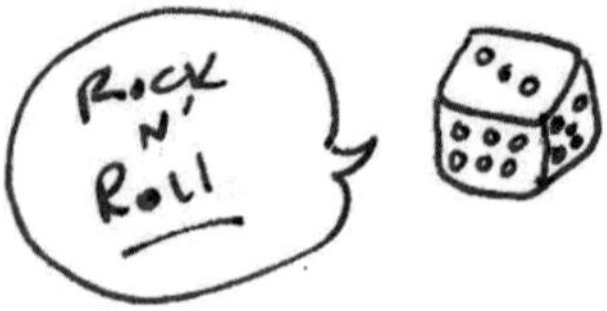
ROCK
N'
ROLL

Your World is Always A Perfect Reflection

Everything happening around you is a MIRROR of your spirit. What you see right now provides you a direct experience to observe.

What do you appreciate in others? That's yours. That is your highest essence and expression. And providing gratitude and acknowledging that in others reflects back to you.

And what about where you might experience others behaving in ways you'd rather not see in your life. Yes, that's a reflection for you too. Each relationship is a way to see ourselves through a mirror. As you become more and more of a clear mirror by purifying your heart, practicing connecting to source and in full love - the mirror gets polished. As you love yourself, others cannot remain in your life who take advantage of you. Or, as you practice forgiveness, others cannot come in who would require forgiveness. Your world is the creation of what's going on inside. Peace or turmoil. Your choices are reflected... perfectly. You are in relationship with the "pieces" of yourself mirrored in multiple angles, ways and people back to you. As Gandhi is famous for saying, " Be the change you wish to see."

WHY DOES THIS MESSAGE MATTER TO YOU TODAY?

_____

_____

_____

_____

_____

_____

How would you want this answer to be different one year from now?

_____

_____

_____

_____

_____

Why DRINKING COULD BE DERAILING YOUR DESTINY of GREATNESS

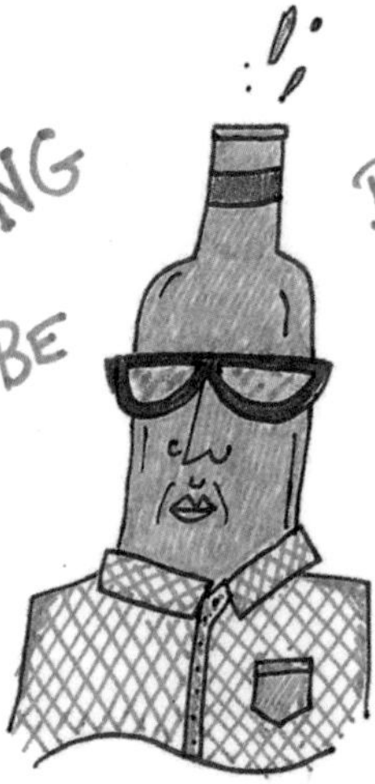

Most highly talented entrepreneurs I know are drinking too much to cover up for their own biggest potential. By drinking and partying we don't have to face our REAL purpose or examine what that greatest expression can truly become. I'm not going to make an "always" or "never" statement here - but if this strikes a nerve or triggers an emotional response, there's something to look at here. «CHEERS!»

A few years back I realized I was drinking too much (at least for me). I couldn't remember one stretch of more than 1-2 consecutive days without a glass of wine, bourbon or beer. It wasn't a lot, but I just couldn't recall a time period of not really drinking. I wanted to see what happened when I stopped. I like experiments and I tried 33 days of no drinking. It really made me see how so many situations have drink woven into them. It was more a habit than anything else but forced me to bring awareness to it. About 3 weeks in I got "amnesia" about the end date. Surely I knew the date but thought I had miscalculated. At midnight on the final night, I had a semi-cold cider on my front steps and realized I was proud of myself for getting through it - but I hadn't changed much. The next summer I tried again, and this time after the 33 days, I did see a greater change around intention. Previously it was more habitual and now there was awareness and even consciousness about drinking. Truly enjoying it if I wanted instead of a default. Like one year on Necker doing shots with Branson. There was a reason to celebrate a big impact project together. But the biggest change for me has been aligning with my greater purpose and true dharma. (The big stuff!) I want to be at my optimal so I don't miss any moments. Full awareness. I've also been paying more attention to subtle aspects, like when I drink I feel less intuitive for 2-3 days.

Each time - I decide is it worth it? Will it enhance my experience now more fully for what I may give up the next period?..

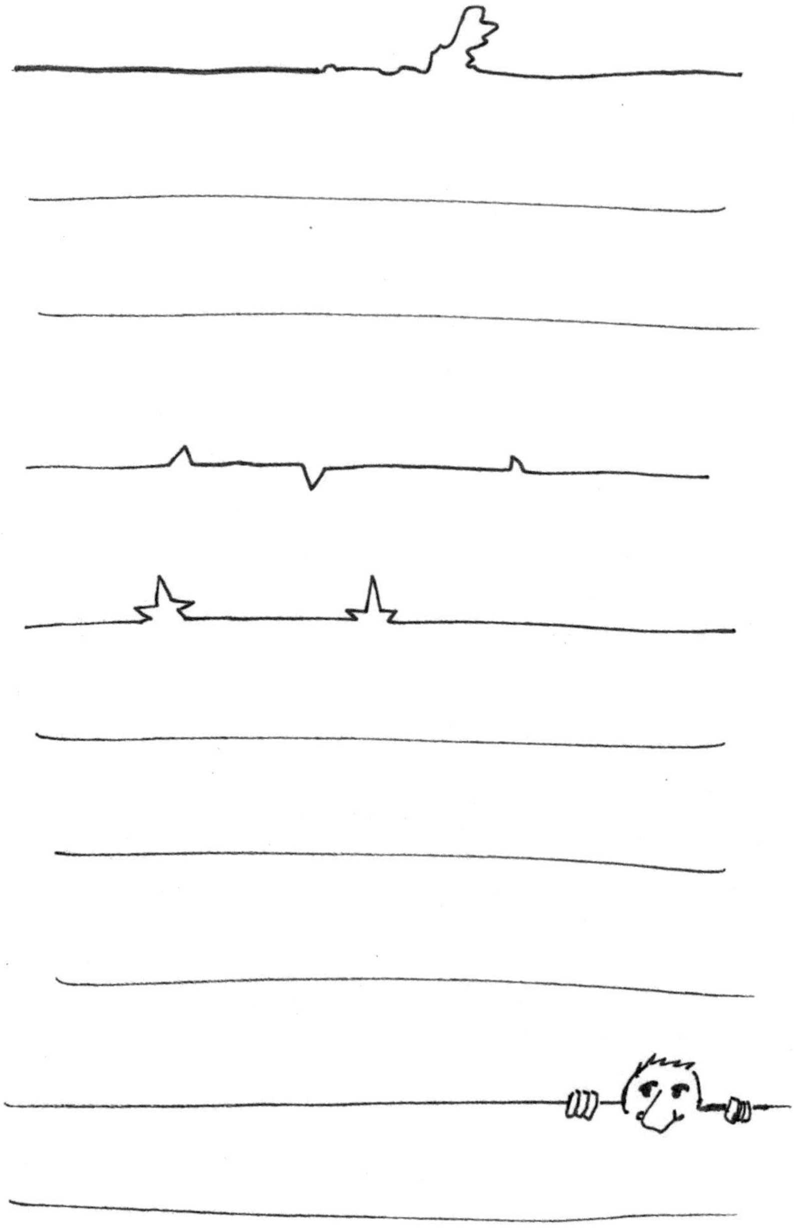

RAinbow
Rules BY ZOE SILVER (AGE 8 1/2)

① Everyone Has
one same power,
following your dreams

② Everyone can Be what they want

③ Everyone is true

④ Don't Give up

⑤ Be Cool

⑥ Do what you want And Show it

⑦ Be Special and Good

Children often are the best truth tellers... I found an old
butterfly journal cleaning out our basement and these are the
Rainbow Rules to live by. I guessed age 8 1/2 but Zoe thought
much younger still. Such beautiful wisdom. They are getting
it from a 'pure' source. Our children are our teachers if we
allow them to share their lessons.

> "All children are born geniuses, and we
> spend the first six years of their lives
> degeniusing them." — R. Buckminster Fuller

Why?*

Why does this page matter to you right now?

(Whatever you answer, keep asking WHY to get deeper and deeper to the real WHY.)

ANSWER #1: _____

_____

_____

Why? _____

_____

_____

Why? _____

_____

_____

Why? _____

_____

_____

Why? _____

_____

_____

Why? _____

_____

_____

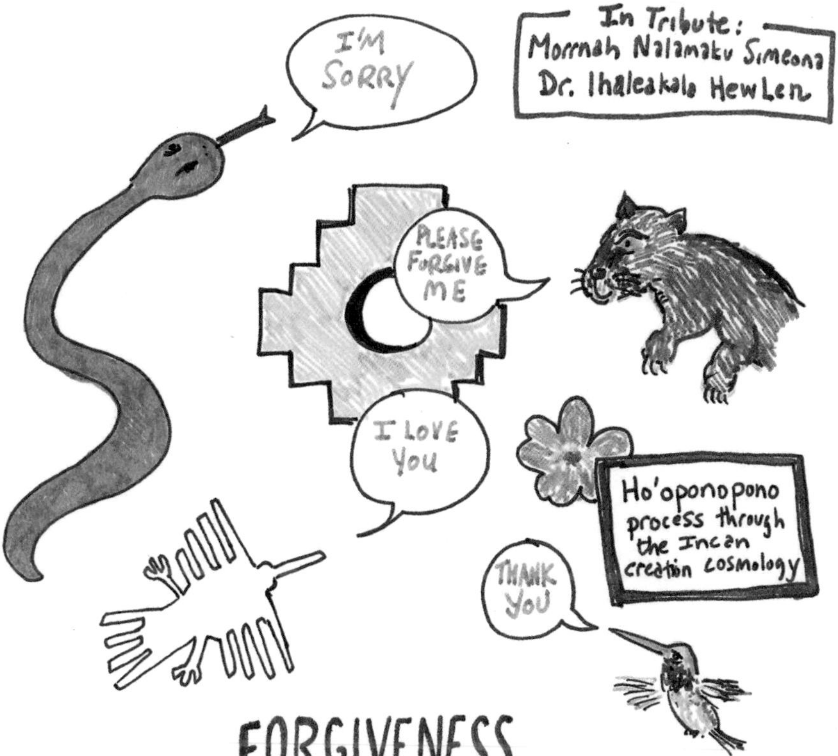
In Tribute:
Morrnah Nalamaku Simeona
Dr. Ihaleakala Hew Len
I'M SORRY
PLEASE FORGIVE ME
I LOVE YOU
Ho'oponopono process through the Incan creation cosmology
THANK YOU

FORGIVENESS

- FORWARD IS FOREVER AND -
FOREVER YOURS

We carry so much guilt and judgement of ourselves that can all be let go with these 4 sentiments expressed with an open heart. Forgiving ourselves cleanses us to also forgive others who we feel have wronged us or those not in alignment with our path. Forgiveness contains an extremely HIGH healing energy vibration. Once you can unblock yourself and release past guilt, you can do the same for others, regardless if you've "met" yet or not. But even higher is THE knowing there doesn't even need to be any forgiveness because we are all perfectly imperfect in divine order.

HOMEWORK ASSIGNMENT:

Write a Love Letter to Yourself from your heart... and mail it. (Seriously)

This is the letter I mailed myself on 7-7-13. It took nearly 2 weeks to arrive and I was wondering what that meant. But the extra time was perfect because opening it back up again, I was almost reading it for the first time all over again. Don't over think it – what would your heart say? Write it all to yourself...

DEAR YANIK -

Congratulations! Everything you have been seeking is yours! I've never written to tell you This but...

I ♥ YOU!

Yes, There are so many reasons I love you. I love you exactly how you are now, for what you're already accomplished and for what is yet to be. I love your creativity, Generosity, ability to spark fun in situations and others. I love how you can come up with incredible ideas on the spot and make them happen. I love the way you aren't afraid to be a bit goofy and keep your inner child alive + well. I love That you are inspiring to others by simply being genuine and authentic. Your life is an adventure – let's experience a truly EPIC journey together. I love that MAGIC happens around you! synchronicities. I love the path you are on to catalyze greatness ... it's not an accident your relationships at the highest levels

I am really in AWE of how you've awakened to a bigger role + destiny you have. I love how you can bring together amazing + diverse individuals who collectively can co-create even more. I love the ARTISTIC spark That's been re-awakened. I'm astounded by the way you can see more interconnected possibilities and a bigger vision for the EcoVerse. I love That you were not content to stay comfortable – but interested in DARING GREATLY... I love the symbols + signs lining up.

MOST of all I SIMPLY LOVE YOU! XOXO

Totally + completely + Forever ⊙ ∞

What do you really + truly admire about yourself? Say it! It's too easy to see our faults – when have you truly highlighted everything great about you?

FROM:
Your Secret ♥ Admirer ♥

GALACTIC

USA

Yep use a real stamp too!

TO: YANIK SILVER
1234 ANY STREET
Everywhere, MILKY WAY
GALAXY

Draw in your letter if you like

Actually mail it. Maybe from a meaningful location too.

Handwrite it even if you hate your handwriting

Set a timer and write non-stop for 6 minutes

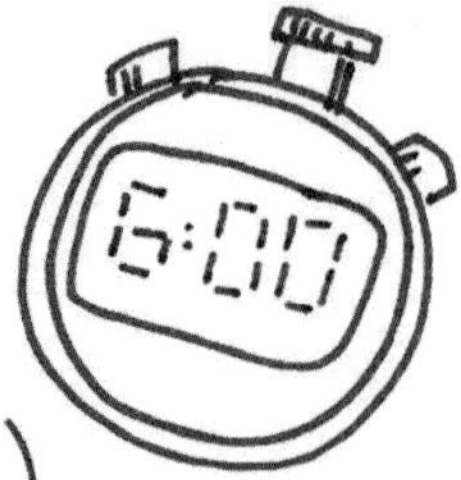
6:00

(no editing + keep your pen moving)

Okay Go

Keep Going

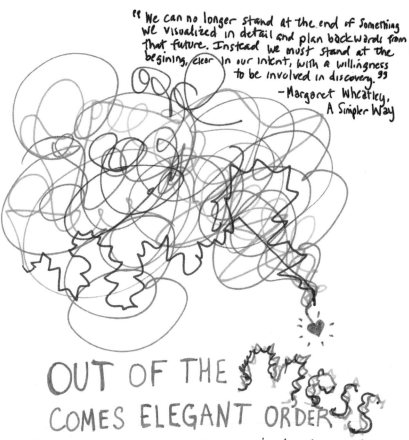

"We can no longer stand at the end of something we visualized in detail and plan backwards from that future. Instead we must stand at the begining, clear in our intent, with a willingness to be involved in discovery."

—Margaret Wheatley, A Simpler Way

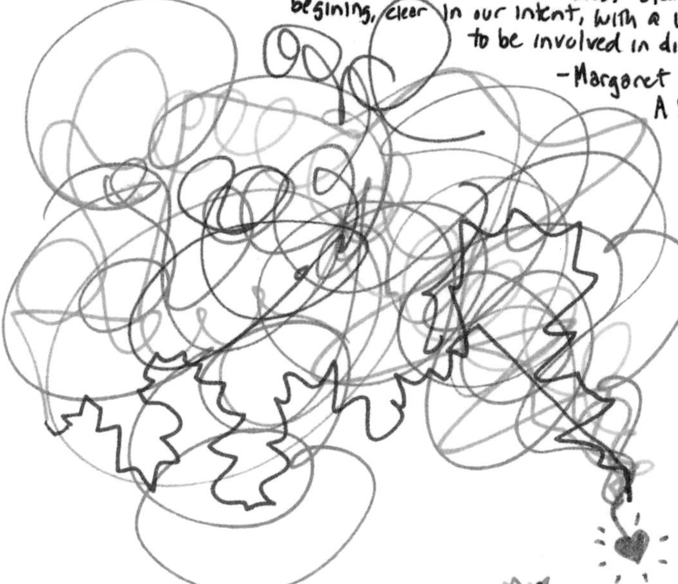

OUT OF THE MESS COMES ELEGANT ORDER

Everything great looks messy in the middle. There is just no straight line to true breakthroughs anymore in your life and business. The "Mess" is organic and expected. It's the mashing up of resources, ideas, deep downloads, signs, synchronicities, chance relationships and incubation time. Not only should you know a mess may be good but also realize the "cooking" time needed. The Ecoverse Thinking of interconnected companies, partners, networks and shared services comes together with each piece perfectly aligning and serving the whole. Ari Weinzweig from Zingerman's tells me the healthiest Ecosystems are the most diverse and complex. Just like organic gardening. Zingermans has built their ZCOB (Zingermans Community of Businesses) from a deli that buys baked goods from their bakery to coffee from the roasting co and uses the training division (ZingTrain) to help culture + the shared services division handles HR, marketing, tech for all the companies. Each one runs as a separate business ~~selling to "built-in" Zingermans customers~~ but also outside.

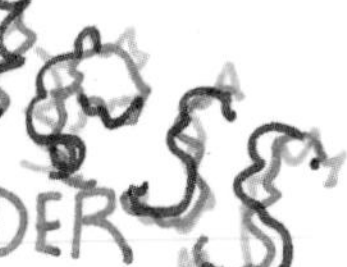

THIS SEEMING MESS CREATED SOMETHING AMAZING!

Smooth Seas Never
made a Skilled Sailor

It's easy when things are going "smooth." But real growth begins when waves appear. You learn a lot about others and yourself. When you encounter obstacles and setbacks, it makes you question is your WHY big enough? When you make it through a storm, you know you can perservere through anything. Everything else seems easy afterwards.

At the first ripples of things not going your way, anything you sorta hoped for or kinda wished for fades away. You're left with what you authentically were designed to accomplish and have a part of. It's your deepest purpose that cannot be swayed or moved from, regardless of the surging sea. At this point you've found bedrock and your home base. This is your safe harbor no one can move you from.

TEXT·A·FRIEND
ROULETTE

Send This entry to a
friend and see what happens.
Or tell Them you were inspired
to send This to Them as an answer
to something They are working on.

Bonus: Try someone you haven't seen in 6 months

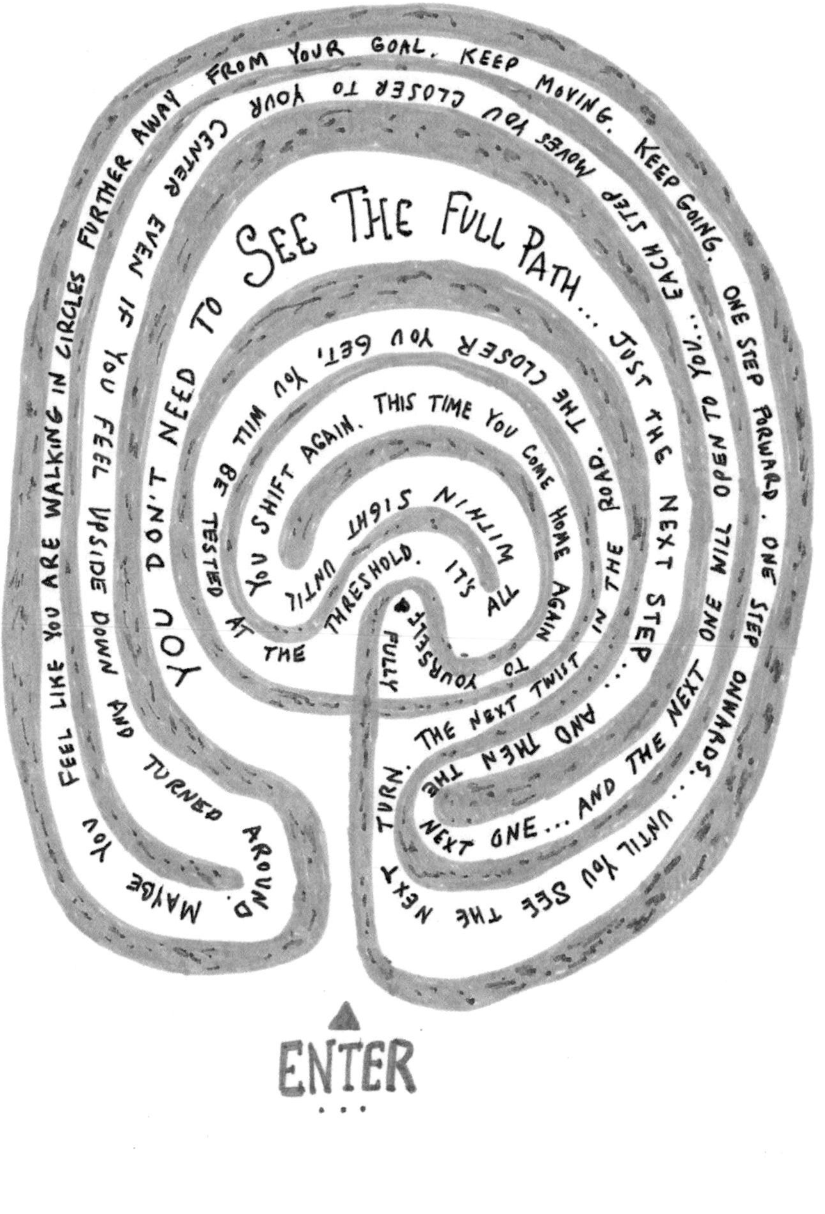
MAYBE YOU FEEL LIKE YOU ARE WALKING IN CIRCLES FURTHER AWAY FROM YOUR GOAL. KEEP MOVING. KEEP GOING. ONE STEP FORWARD. ONE STEP ONWARDS... UNTIL YOU SEE THE NEXT TURN.
AND THEN THE NEXT ONE... AND THE NEXT ONE WILL OPEN TO YOU... EACH STEP MOVES YOU CLOSER TO YOUR CENTER EVEN IF YOU FEEL UPSIDE DOWN AND TURNED AROUND.
YOU DON'T NEED TO SEE THE FULL PATH... JUST THE NEXT STEP... THE NEXT TWIST IN THE ROAD.
THE CLOSER YOU GET, YOU WILL BE TESTED AT THE THRESHOLD. IT'S ALL WITHIN SIGHT UNTIL YOU SHIFT AGAIN. THIS TIME YOU COME HOME AGAIN TO YOURSELF FULLY.
ENTER
...

Why?

Why does this page matter to you right now?

(Whatever you answer, keep asking WHY to get deeper and deeper to the real WHY.)

ANSWER #1: _____

_____

_____

Why?

_____

_____

_____

Why?

_____

_____

_____

Why?

_____

_____

_____

Why?

_____

_____

_____

Why?

_____

_____

Ask
Wonderfully
Receive
Graciously

For so many of us, we find it easier to give than to receive. There's an infinite circuit of both that are required for you. It's like breathing—you cannot simply exhale only ... or even inhale forever. That would be silly but why do we believe This natural rhythm doesn't apply in This other way too?

We are all wired to get deep satisfaction + happiness from giving to someone else. And as you receive, you allow that person to also experience the same. Why not ASK wonderfully ... full of cheerful expectation? Others want to provide for you. The Universe is ready to oblige in alignment with your greater purpose.

Receive with grace... The grace of knowing you deserve joyful abundance with full appreciation and an overflowing heart of gratitude. Like magic! It's a full circle...

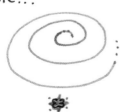

Ha-Ha-Ha-Ha...

What's the cosmic joke here?

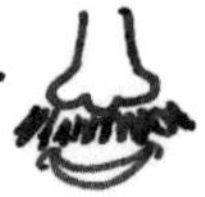

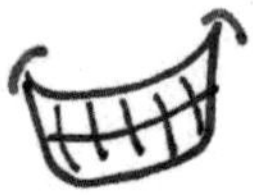

THIS WAY TO
Love, Laughter
& HAPPILY
Ever After

What gives you love, laughter + happiness
is where your energy naturally flows in
a state of joyful expression.

Each day ensure you are checking in on
that "simple" benchmark - and ensure you are
adding to it.

Your journal is also your path to being
continually supported... It's for you and
also those who are awakening with you.

TURN up the LIGHTS & BRIGHTNESS
of the VISION

Hey –
You called?

Write down __15__ things you're grateful for right now:

(1) _____

(2) _____

(3) _____

(4) _____

(5) _____

(6) _____

(7) _____

(8) _____

(9) _____

(10) _____

(11) _____

(12) _____

(13) _____

(14) _____

(15) _____

Hint: Specific Things
What's around you now?
What in this entry reminded you of something?

I saw This Love Spray street art by Con$umer in New York - and it inspired me to draw what I was grateful for...

Continuing to light the path by walking the path
Mentors - Richard - Frank - Hshale
1000 SUNS
Books appearing at the right time
Flight upgrade
Caps in playoffs
I AM on your SIDE
158 lbs
John sending Gummy bears
Ocean Impact 30x30
Returning to Ulusaba
Chiefs in championship
80% Plant
Colleagues seeing success + platform building
Cheer w/ Zoe
Zoe about being positive
ART in Journal
·Daily drawings
Meditation 4yrs YOGA
Outdoor Ed w/ Zack
I AM
Virgin Galactic powered flight
LOVE SPRAY
CAUTION
CONTENTS MAY INDUCE JOY
Cherry Blossoms w/Missy
Safari business sessions
Make Magic
Breakfast w/Missy
+Zack
Perfect unfolding of cosmic Story
Heart opening
More + more clues each day
YES
Camp Theme
Planning for TLC
teaching more + more journaling
Stabilo Pens

Being grateful connects deeply + fully with the source of all blessings. It's too easy to take Things for granted. Instead take a moment to truly see + pay attention to what you are grateful for and appreciate... big + small...

It's also too easy to see "What's wrong," which only magnifies and pulls more attention to what you don't want. Appreciate and give thanks even for the Things, issues, people & situations you want to change. Coat with Love Spray! Apply several applications - across everything!

WHO ELSE NEEDS TO HEAR
THIS MESSAGE TODAY?

(Hint: By teaching an idea, you deepen your understanding and knowing)

WHO?
_____

What happened?
_____
_____
_____

WHO?
_____

What happened?
_____
_____
_____

WHO?
_____

What happened
_____
_____
_____

#COSMICJOURNAL

PLAY

IS CALLED

RE/CREATION

for a reason...

Play is one of our most natural expressions of WHO we are in our perfected states. Joy and play are totally inter-woven together. And joy is your path back home. When you have the choice between two options, consider what brings out more play? More joy? When we play there is a youthful energy and spark to us that can be seen by everyone. As adults we've gotten too serious. When you allow the little boy or girl inside of you to PLAY, magic happens. The word "RECREATION" gives us a clue about the power of play. The words are RE.Creation because it "re-creates" our world.

⊛

We are naturally drawn to play if we simply give ourselves permission to explore how to play, what we loved as kids, and how to add more of it to our lives & work! you need to set an appointment for yourself. A PLAYDATE! Have you ever been around someone who is simply playing? Quite frankly, our work doesn't need to feel like... well, work. Perhaps that is what we are meant to be doing down here on Earth... playing more!

> "... the opposite of PLAY is not work — the opposite of PLAY is depression."
> — Stuart Brown

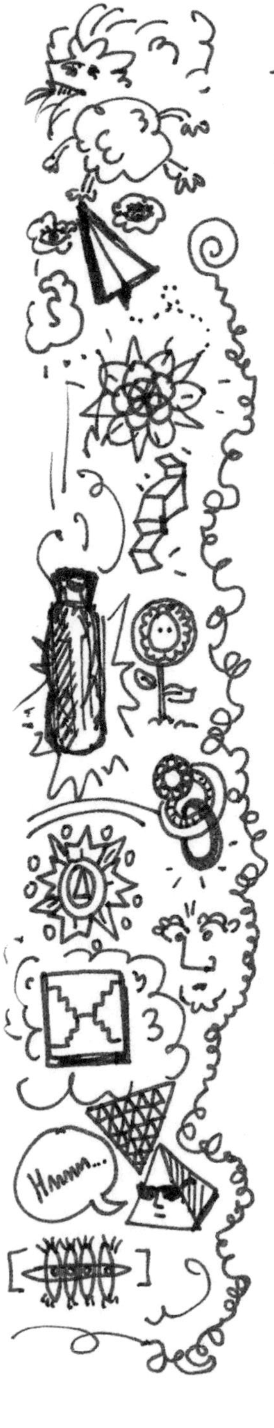
Hmmm...

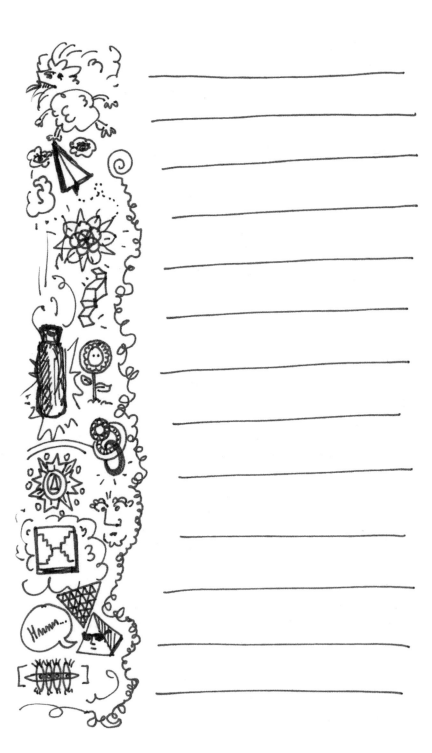

Make Magic

Driving the kids to look at Summer Camps, I was explaining a little about how when you set an intention, it shows up, almost like MAGIC. The kids didn't really believe me so we started easy. They asked for a dog and a horse. Simple! We saw those within 30 minutes. Now we were ready for a challenge. Missy said a "penguin." okay, great... I was confident we'd see, just a matter of how. I didn't have to wait too long. ~~At~~ The second camp we visited, the kids went out and played while the parents got the tour. We only walked into one bunk and right on a dresser was a piece of art just like this... from one of the campers

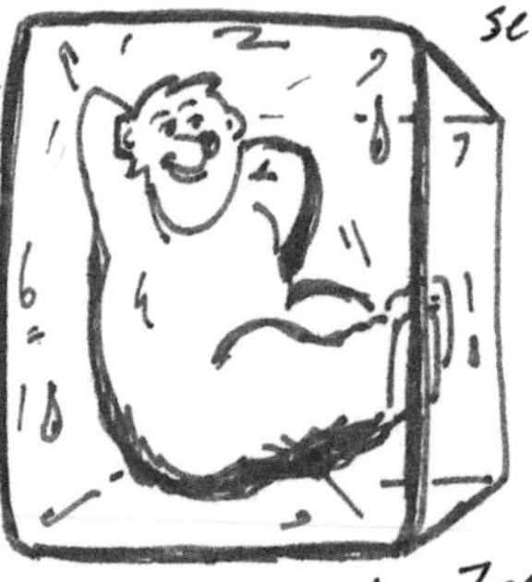

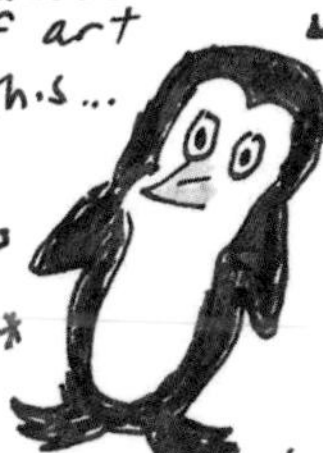

Missy couldn't believe it! On the way home we talked about it, and now the kids got BOLDER! Zoe asked to see a polar bear, and I said an ice cube. Hmmm... once again I just knew it'd show up, but I'd have to see in what wondrous way. The main highway was at a standstil, and after slowly winding through traffic, I found an alternative exit to get off. We were in the car so long, everyone needed a break. There was only 1 Quick-mart type store, and as we walked in, on the ice cooler was Zoe's Polar bear and not only that but my ice cube, all entangled together. PERFECT! Her jaw dropped in amazement, and this became one of the "Make MAGIC" stories they'll always remember.

Now it seems like there is always a little bit of doubt when MAGIC happens. "Don't all ice coolers have this bear?" No they don't. But enough that we sometimes question what just happened. I prefer this way...

"There are only two ways to live your life. One is as though nothing is a miracle. The other is as though everything is a miracle."

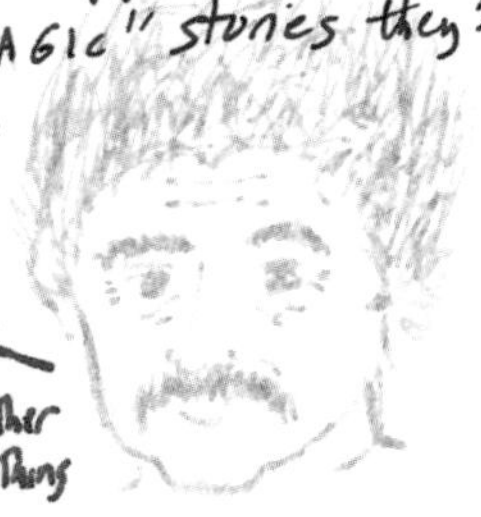

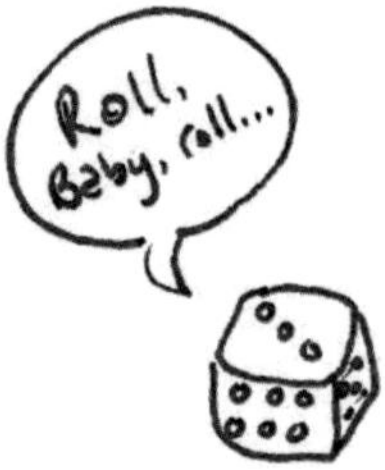
Roll,
Baby, roll...

Synchronicity *

IS A

Love Letter

FROM THE

UNIVERSE

ACROSS TIME & SPACE

Hello!
All the Signs
Symbols, Colors,
Songs + nudges are
meant for you to
know you have a
direct connection
to Source.
Just Re-remember

Assignment:
Keep a note with all the
synchronicities you've
experienced. Is there a pattern?
What opens up when you see
the list? Make Magic *

So What do you think?

Really?

DOORS WILL OPEN

FOR YOU WHERE

THERE WERE ONLY WALLS

Artist
inspiration:
Jennifer Verse

Joseph
Campbell

Follow
Your Bliss

Following your "bliss" is so powerful yet also misunderstood.
It's not just what makes us happy. That's fleeting... like an
ice cream sundae. Your true bliss is joyful service and full
utilization of everything you were designed to do here. That's when
doors open for you. It's almost like magic how events and
circumstances align for your benefit... almost out of nowhere.
You find that bliss by your excitement level. What inspires you?
What you're magnetically attracted to is not an accident. By
having faith the unrelated pieces will connect, simply because
of your connection to them. Or you can continue banging your
head against the walls placed purposely in front of you for
not following your authentic path + true destiny. These walls
are there to keep bumping you back into your ultimate decision.
To simply do what you would do anyway if you got no
acclaim, no rewards, no fame, no wealth or even benefits from
it except your own Love, joy and bliss. That's your greatest
"return" on your greatest work of your life... ₤KNOCK
₤ KNOCK₤

107

THREE

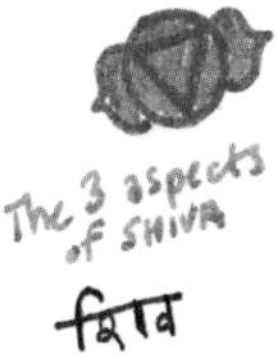

The 3 aspects of SHIVA
शिव

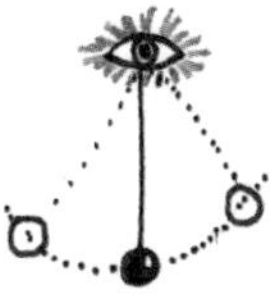

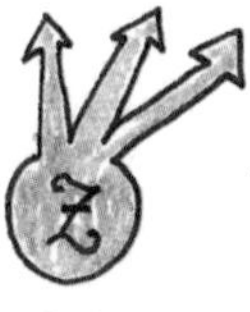

At the Third point, you get elevated beyond the two polarities and back and forth. You can rise above and see the middle way.

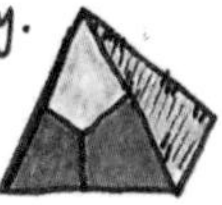

The triangle is one of the most efficient and strongest cosmic structures. Triangles as part of other larger triangles build more complex structures.

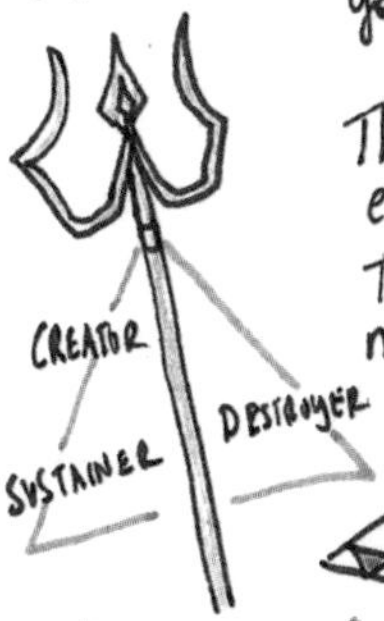

CREATOR
SUSTAINER
DESTROYER

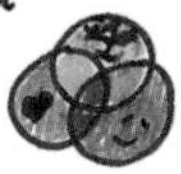

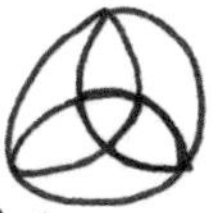

The three primary colors create our color spectrum.

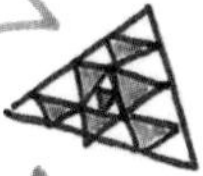

Three provides the perfect interconnectivity of the multiple trinities and combinations. This structure is used for stability and cross-definition.

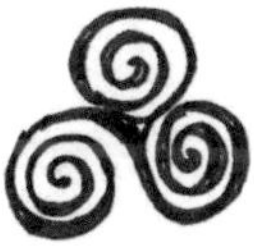

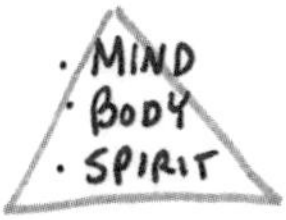

· MIND
· BODY
· SPIRIT

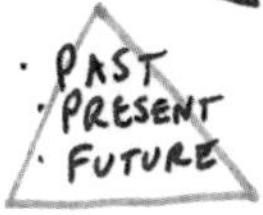

· PAST
· PRESENT
· FUTURE

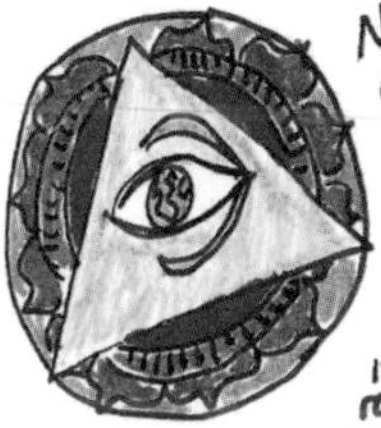

Nearly all ancient cultures taught the idea of another set of vision - the Third Eye. To see in a different way, see through the illusions in this world. It's interesting to me to research the biological aspect of the pineal gland and your other eyes.

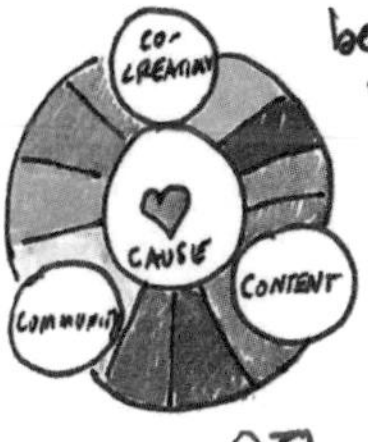

CO-CREATION
CAUSE
CONTENT
COMMUNITY

The EcoVerse could be used for other "Universe Creators"

♥ Cause in center
YOUR WHY —
Content
+ Community
+ Cocreation
— ΔΔΔ —

1. The content is education, media, training, etc - This builds your
2. community. You have the sandbox for like-minded people to come together and stand for something more in alignment with the cause - and together
3. Co-create new ideas, projects, co-op initiatives that the community can support and develop

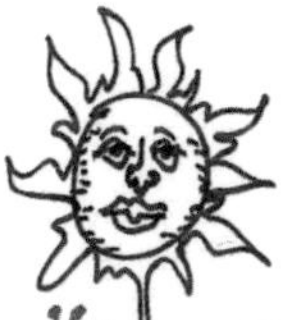

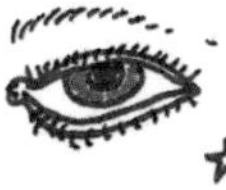

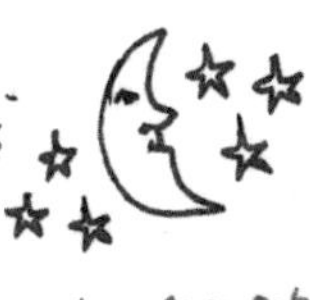

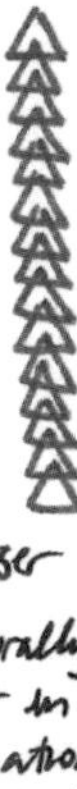

"Genius is the ability to make connections and see potential where others don't (and for it to be totally natural.)"
- Rebecca Alban Hoffberger

CONNECT
CATALYZE
CO-CREATE

What are three things you can combine (naturally) to be a genius? You don't have to be the best in the ~~world~~ at each of the three - just the combination.

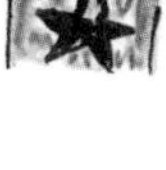

Hamilton was a hit by Lin Manuel Miranda, combining hip-hop / musicals + history. Not in a contrived way - but because he loved it all!

My friend Jordan Guernsey said cancer was his greatest gift... and that he never had a bad day in his life.

Jordan was one of my favorite people, and I got to know him for too short of a time. Jordan was a Maverick member, and although we spent time together, we never connected more deeply until he was diagnosed with late-stage melanoma. We had so many great adventures, simply embracing, loving life + PLAYING! As things progressed, he kept a few friends up to date. One day he tells me **FYI** he thought things were close. This is coming from a man who had truly transformed in so many ways — so him telling this wasn't an indication of giving up, but rather it felt more like an ...invitation...

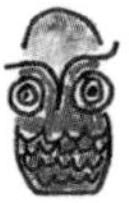

3 WISHES

1. FORGIVE FREELY
2. LOVE UNCONDITIONALLY
3. WISH FOR UNLIMITED WISHES

—JORDAN GUERNSEY'S Final 3 Wishes

Listen to the interview: YanikSilver.com/LightInside

On December 8, 2014, Jordan Guernsey headed off on his next cosmic Adventure. He was only 30 years old.

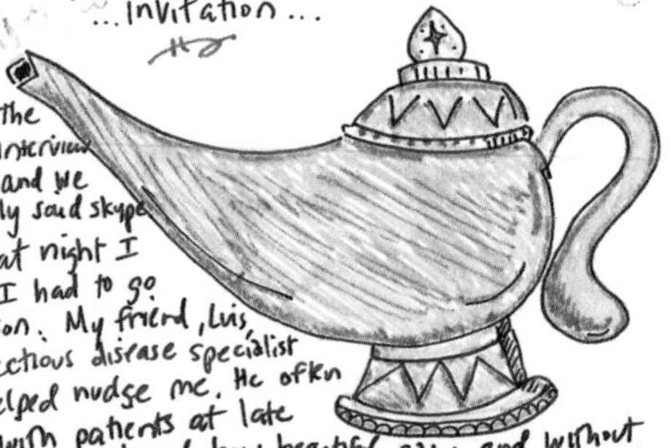

I had the idea to interview Jordan and we tentatively said Skype. But that night I knew I had to go in person. My friend, Luis, an infectious disease specialist really helped nudge me. He often works with patients at late stages and he shared how beautiful, raw and without pretense everything is at this point. This was the setup for the first {LEGENDARY LEGACY} interview to honor Jordan's life as an entrepreneur and more importantly an incredible, loving human. Now I've had the privilege of interviewing some of the biggest business icons, celebrities + thought leaders, and I've never relistened to any of them. This one I've listened to multiple times because we got into a meaningful deep dive... Entheogens, mushrooms, love, work, how to say goodbye, why cancer was his greatest gift + more! Jordan's neighbor dropped by and asked him to do something when he passes so he knows he's not really gone. He suggested making their local pro soccer team, Real Salt Lake, win the championship. Jordan said, "No. Instead I will be the wind blowing your hair, the magnificent stars + sun... and the whiff of weed." HA. Jordan never lost his sense of humor through everything. And as I left that day, there was no big overwhelming goodbye. We just hugged like normal and said, "I love you... and see you soon."

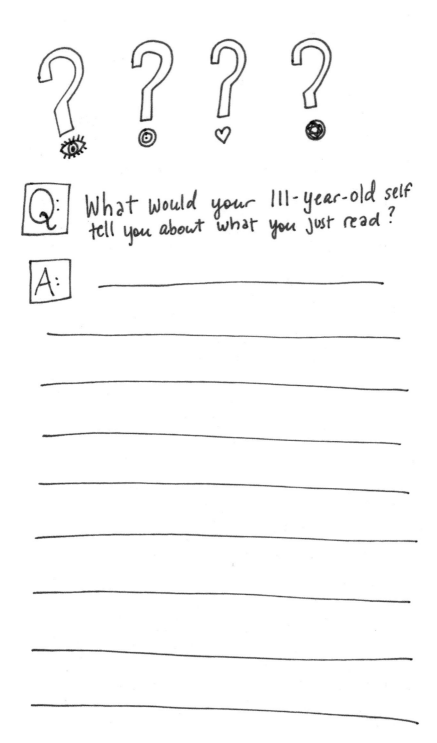

Q: What would your 111-year-old self tell you about what you just read?

A: _____

_____

_____

_____

_____

_____

_____

_____

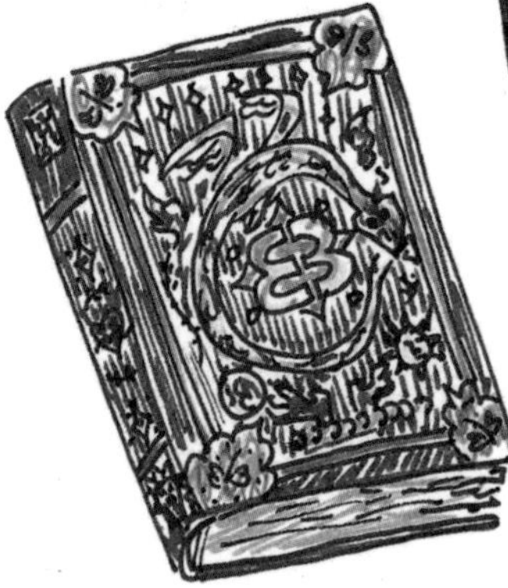

WRITE YOUR NEXT ·GREATEST· Chapter

Allow everything perfectly because it's already perfect. You're simply Re-Remembering that perfection. It's time...

There is something BIG brewing –
can you feel it?

The pieces, people, resources, all lining up for you to carry out your soul's greatest expression coming through you as a conduit. Co-create an evolutionary acceleration by catalyzing the catalysts...who can change the way business is played!

There's no denying it's happening – can't you feel it rippling out of you? Allow it fully... trust the divine timing of this next chapter... connect to your heart resonance for the highest collective purpose.

Allow all your gifts and talents. feeling fully & totally alive, joyfully receive all the ensuing "rewards." Allow yourself to be a steward for larger and larger impacts, investments, relationships, opportunities and connections. Not doubting or discounting your unique contribution (even if it's coming "easy" to you). Rising in fullness to your destiny unfolding here. A destiny of greatness to have a true global impact – not because "you" are so great but because the vision you have "downloaded" from SOURCE demands it. Your full + total effortless effort aligned with a deeper knowing and imprint. A knowing, not a belief even. A knowing to fulfill the COSMIC GALACTIC plan because you dreamt and wrote that plan already. What you long for is deeply longing for you to bring it forth.

The signs, symbols and synchronicities are trail markers

Why?*

Why does this page matter to you right now?

(Whatever you answer, keep asking WHY to get deeper and deeper to the real WHY.)

ANSWER #1: _____

_____

_____

Why?

_____

_____

_____

Why?

_____

_____

_____

Why?

_____

_____

_____

Why?

_____

_____

_____

Why?

_____

_____

DARE.
Greatly!

What would be felt 300 years from now? Your greatest work stands the power of the centuries. What are you doing that will truly create your legendary legacy?

D - DISCOVER: Discover what you are uniquely designed to do here. Your greatest journey is truly understanding your divine combination of skills, talents, natural attributes, past experiences, etc.

A - ACTIVATE: Activate your unique genius. Stand in your voice and power of who you were meant to be. Accelerate it, step forward and proclaim your place.

R - RE·Remember: RE·Remember WHO you are... A perfect and infinite spiritual being experiencing this time + space... because you chose it for your growth. RE·Remember your true mission here... why you came.

E - EVOLVE: Take your biggest dream for the greatest collective · and follow it. What is your NEXT chapter that will dwarf everything up to this point... utilizing what you've already built and achieved?

TEXT· ROULETTE

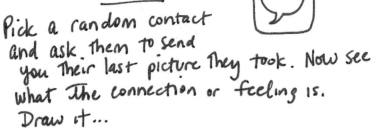

Pick a random contact
and ask them to send
  you their last picture they took. Now see
what the connection or feeling is.
Draw it...

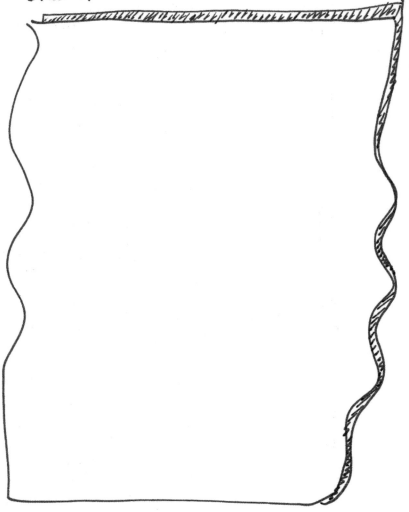

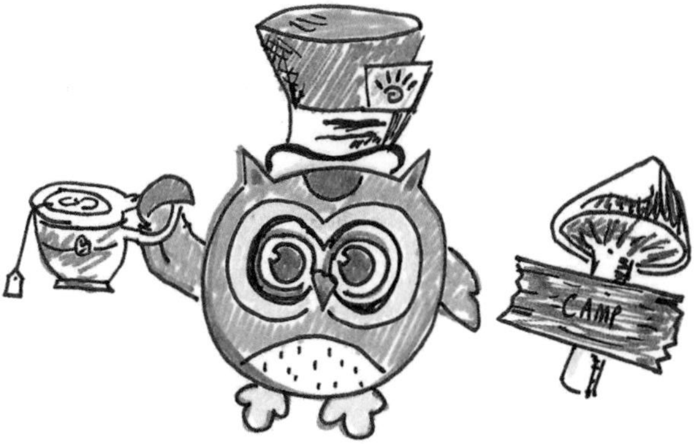
CAMP

WE'RE ALL MAD HERE...

You have to be a bit (or alot) bonkers, mad, or crazy in the greatest way possible to accomplish something that really matters. The easiest thing is to let others criticize or not support your wild ideas. It takes your own internal total knowing to be strong - so it doesn't matter what anyone else says, believes or does that isn't in support of your vision. You only look MAD until it works. Then others could see it all along.

The biggest innovators, rule breakers, disruptors and rabble rousers were all bonkers... and then they slowly found a few others who also thought like this, and a few more and more. Until they came together to support each other for their wildest ideas with the potential for the greatest impact because they finally found their tribe of trouble makers!

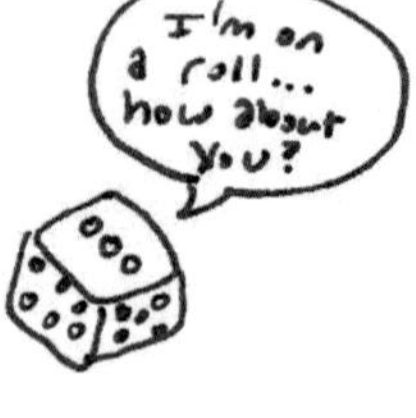
I'm on a roll... how about you?

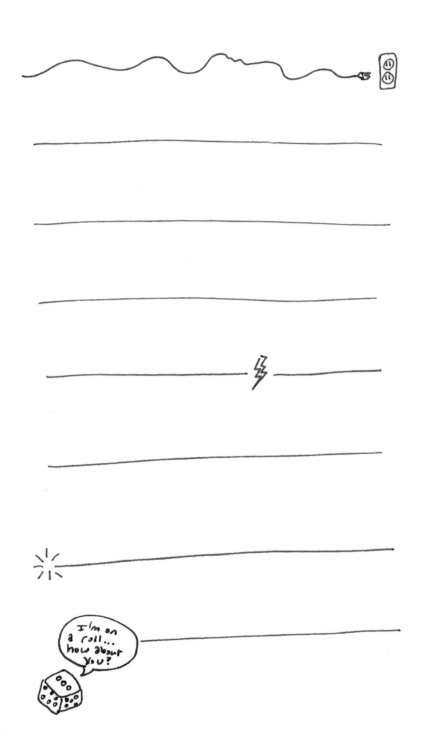

A Light can only Grow Brighter BY Lighting Another & Lighting Another... AND Another...

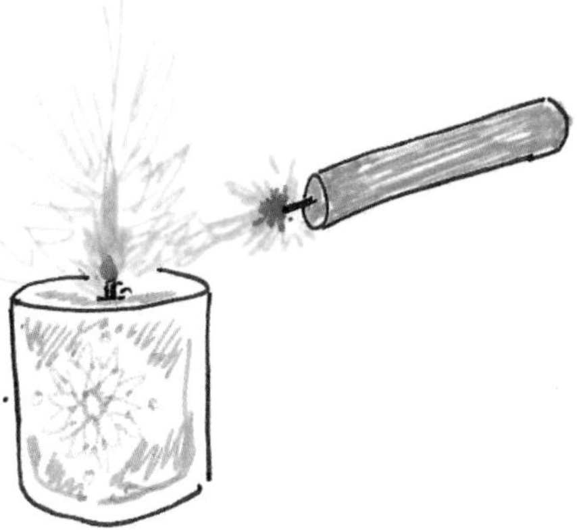

No matter how much you may try, you cannot diminish a light by lighting more lights. Our lights grow brighter and brighter with every spark, flame, fire, inferno or super nova ignited. One light can spread through a family, community, city, company or even the galaxy. Light only grows + expands.

Lighting another's fire may be teaching, encouraging, providing comfort or serving. Take teaching... Some people believe if they teach they reduce their chances of the same idea or tactic working for them again. Not true. Teaching enables you to light so many other candles that you are then able to see your next steps on the evolutionary path. It opens up a space for you to step through into what's NEXT...

There's something perfect about evolving and growing through teaching and lighting the next group to help alight your way forward.

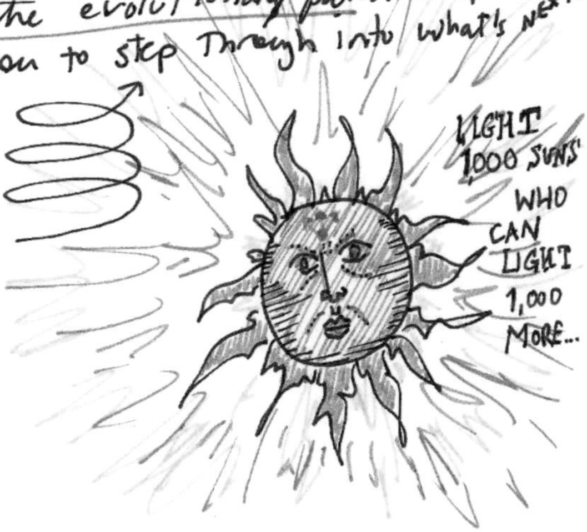
LIGHT
1000 SUNS
WHO
CAN
LIGHT
1,000
MORE...

What are
your
6 WORDS
on your
    tombstone?

___

BORN

*And try writing 6 more
 with your non-dominant hand
 and see if it changes:

_____   _____

_____   _____

_____   _____

<u>BONUS:</u>
Ask 3 friends if these words sound like you.

'Remember Death'

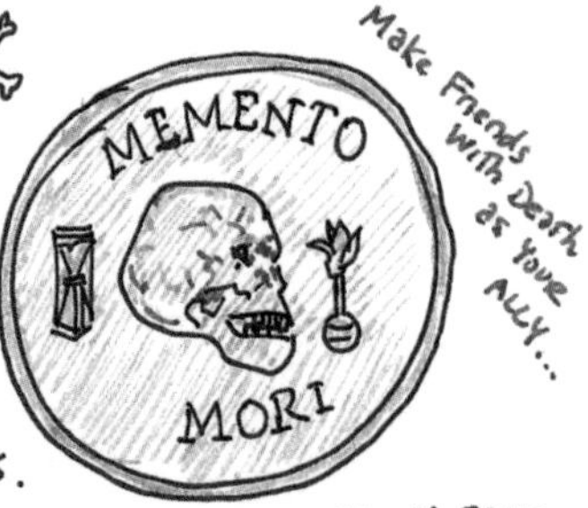
MEMENTO
MORI
Make Friends with Death as your Ally...

That's the Translation of Memento MORI. My friend, Ryan Holiday, had given me this coin last time I saw him in DC. Sounds so cheerful - but there is a realization that nothing is permanent. Everything (physical) dies. Monks have meditated on death for centuries, sometimes going so far as to have actual bones around them. I've meditated in cemeteries before to be a little closer to seeing the fleeting time we have here. Thinking of death is not morbid, it can actually be surprisingly motivating.

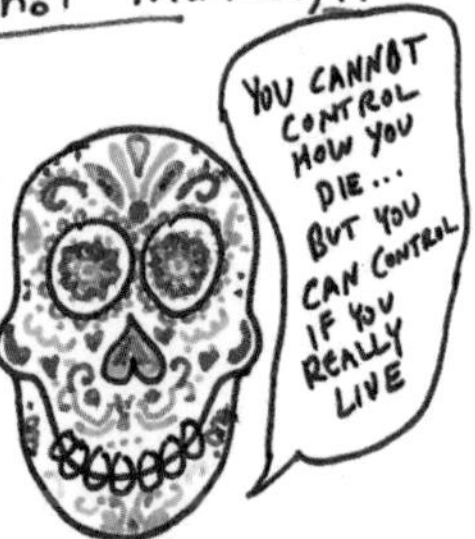
YOU CANNOT CONTROL HOW YOU DIE... BUT YOU CAN CONTROL IF YOU REALLY LIVE

Having an unknown expiration date means we need to consider if we are doing what we are meant to be. There may not be a "Someday." You probably have friends, family or colleagues who have been taken suddenly. Or perhaps someone who was given very little chance of making it and they've beat the odds. How many of them are the same as before? Why do we need something so dramatic to shake our life upside down?

I know some of my friends who keep a countdown clock reminding them time could be running out. The luxury of unlimited time is not ours. Now it definitely doesn't mean you go out + "Hustle" & "Grind" 24/7 because you feel a tick tock in your head.

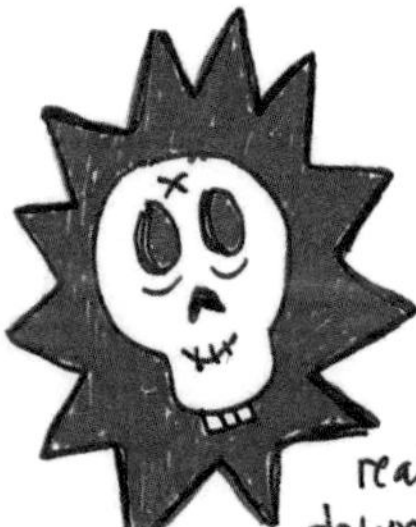

Simply consider if this was your last day, would you be content?

I was on a plane recently and the turbulence was really bad. Now I didn't really think we were going down, but it made me give a little consideration. Had I really done what I was meant to do here? Thankfully my answer was 90% yes. That's a good sign - but there is still even more room for greater alignment. Only you truly know your answer.

As Wayne Dyer would say, "Don't Die With Your Music Still Inside You"

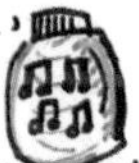

And at the same time realize what you are doing, building, worrying about, etc. is not moving beyond death.

Everything FADES except what is REAL...♥

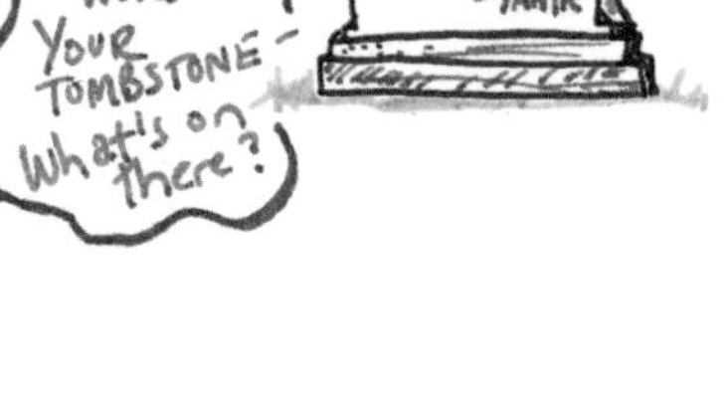
WHAT IF YOU ONLY HAVE 6 WORDS ON YOUR TOMBSTONE - What's on there?
CATALYZING THE CATALYSTS
CONNECTING THE CONNECTORS
-YANIK

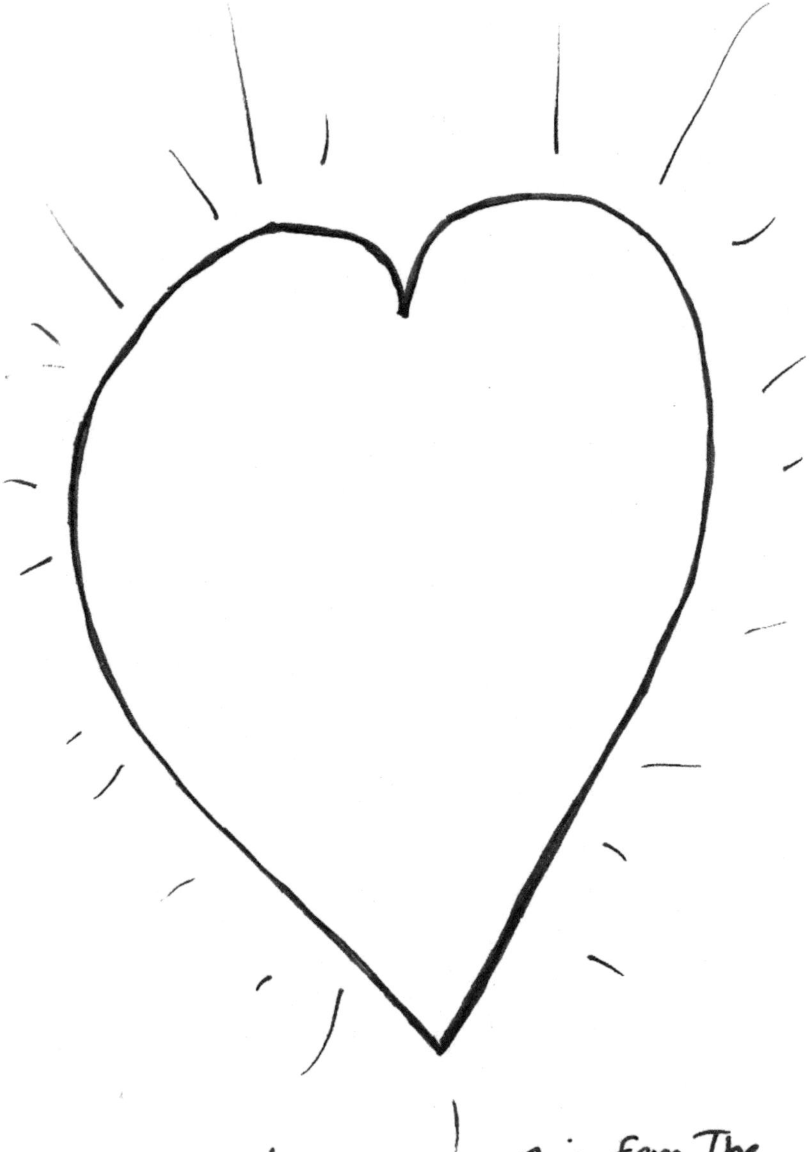

How would you apply this from the greatest expression of LOVE?

HEART OPEN

WHAT NEEDS TO DIE... FOR SOMETHING GREATER TO BE BORN?

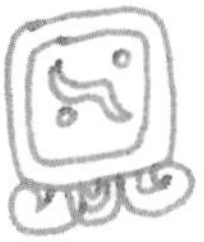
CIMI

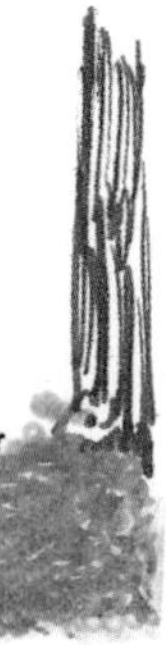

The natural cycles of life go from birth to death to rebirth. But we do not need to die a physical death in order to see a rebirth. It's an intentional "death" and surrender in order to have something even greater emerge...

The Mayan sign of Cimi symbolizes death, and the color is forest green. The forest is constantly in the cycle of life, death and rebirth - creating a beautiful order. Death as our collective ally asks you to cut away outgrown parts of you, your business and your life that no longer serve you. There's a natural vacuum that occurs when you create space.

LET GO

Initially let go what is <u>not</u> needed for you anymore or you'll be forced to let go forcefully. Be willing to do this with intention and open eyes. Fully surrender. Let go and open new pathways for your bigger story to be written and lived. Think of any massive "death" you've had like illness, divorce, failure, seperation, etc. It allows you to become anew. Stagnation builds up the catalyzing force that will create change, one way or another.

"STOP FUCKING AROUND"

—THE UNIVERSE

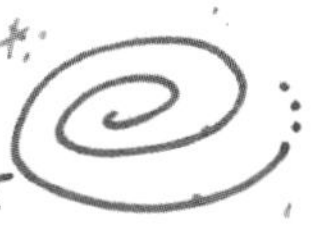

So...

The Universe Always TESTS How Committed You Are

A hope or wish quickly fades when there is adversity. Only a deep commitment to something

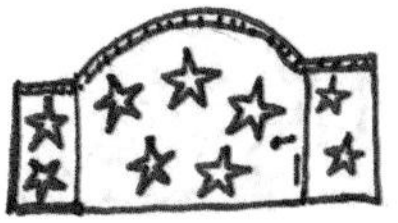

BIGGER

makes you stronger and immune to anything that gets in the way of your task here. Your resolution is constantly tested. Why do New Year's resolutions seem to only last for a moment? The missing piece is the deep... WHY ...The Greater Meaning.

Jack Canfield, who co-authored the Chicken Soup for the Soul series, tells the story of being rejected by publishers 144 times! He kept going because he knew the impact this book of inspirational stories could have. And he was right beyond their wildest dreams... That first Chicken Soup for the Soul book was a big success and the series has gone on to sell over 500 million books!

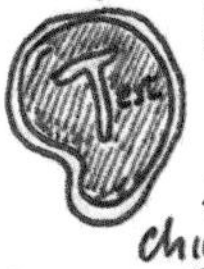
Test

My latest "experiment" was to stop eating meat for 33 days. Tonight was day #18, and our family was invited to dinner at a new friend's house. I noticed the only things on the grill were steaks, chicken, burgers, and hot dogs. Yikes! It had taken us so long to get this dinner scheduled, and they had gone to all this trouble and expense - they were nice steaks - so I thought I should just eat meat. The "test" here was speaking fully in front of people I like. Now I'm not kicking myself or that upset. But I do find it interesting because my resolve for so many other experiments stuck: no sugar, meditation, no drinking, etc. Not sure my own WHY was big enough here since I had already gone to an 80/20 pescatarian diet and didn't really think I'd see a big difference with no meat. But really that's just an excuse... and one is as good as the next.

My own biggest breakthroughs happened after I committed to following through, no matter what. When I was training for a triathlon 2 years back, I made time every day (rain or shine) to workout. And finishing was a huge HIGH-FIVE I gave myself. In fact, even creating this illustrated journal right now is part of a "must-do" 108-day commitment I made to myself, even if tired or traveling. #53/108

Those promises we make to ourselves are the easiest to break or they can be the ones that grow our own self-worth.

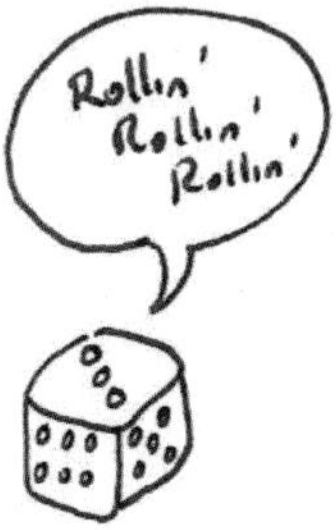
Rollin' Rollin' Rollin'

"BURN" YOUR TEACHERS

Through books, seminars and personal relationships, you may be fortunate to meet and connect with people you look up to, can learn from and even potentially become mentored. One of my earliest influences taught me to pay more attention to the "message" because most messengers were flawed. Separate one from the other.

I've been fortunate to do just that but also look for those individuals who truly walk their talk - not just when they're "on stage" but when nobody is looking too. That's one of my greatest joys: to build true relationships with these types of mentors.

The fact is if you are drawn to any type of teacher, "hero" or "guru", there's a resonance. A type of "Golden Shadow," where their best qualities or attributes <u>you appreciate most are actually yours at your highest expression of who you truly are.</u> Many times that creates attachment by putting someone on a pedestal and their approval carrying more weight for you.

This can happen at every level of teacher - but even more when you really look up to them. My friend Sheryl Netzky is a shaman, and in her training she shared with me the idea they have of "burning their teachers." Appreciating the wisdom, insights and learnings but being WHOLE on your own. I immediately got it. I had been waiting for some sort of "official" acknowledgment from one mentor. I thought I wasn't attached to it - but when I had a rebuff of a request, I realized I was. Sheryl giving me this teaching helped me see I <u>already had all the archetypes</u> imprinting on me that I appreciated in this person.

Once that happened, the very evening I received more kudos and public compliments than ever before. The funny thing is I didn't need them anymore. Of course, I was grateful but it came from a different place. The place of <u>WHOLENESS & INTEGRATION</u>.

YOU ALREADY KNOW THE ANSWER

(But humor me + write it here)

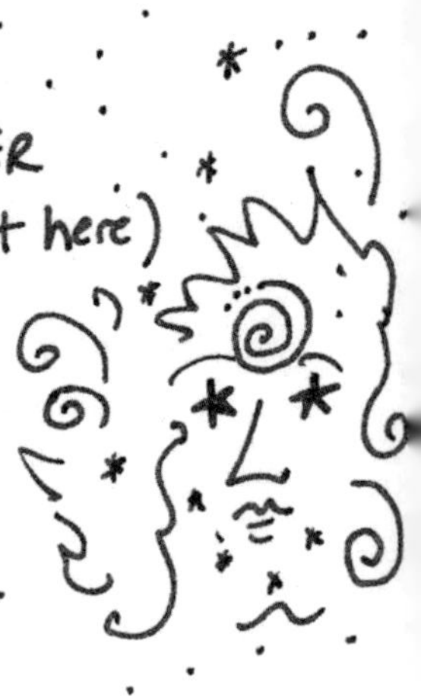

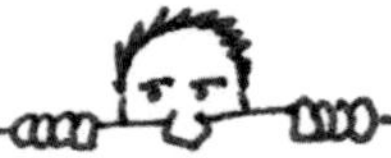

HELLO
my name is

Your Destiny

Names have power. Do you like gooseberries? Not sure? They are now called kiwi fruit. How about a delicious dish of Patagonian Toothfish? Mmm... Actually you know it better as Chilean sea bass. Certain Tribes in Africa + The Amazon give new names to people as they go through certain stages in life. Most people in the West know Mohandas Gandhi by the name "Mahatma," meaning "great soul," as Rabindranath Tagore called him.

NAME

Is there something deeper behind the meaning of your name? My wife goes by Missy - but her full name is Melissa, which means "honey bee." Ironically, she dislikes bees because she worries about being stung. It might not be a coincidence I've been working to help bees + pollinators. I'm fascinated by the way certain names reveal an almost mythic aspect to someone. In the book Change Your Thoughts - Change Your Life, Wayne Dyer explained that his name held a code to his deep connection to the TAO TE CHING. The TAO is "the Way" and Te means adding light or color to the Way. His name, Wayne contains the word "way," and a "dyer" adds color to things. This connection invited Wayne to live out all 81 verses of the Tao one year.

There's an archetype energy in names too. Richard Branson told me during a fireside chat in South Africa that his family name might have been "Brandson"; he really connected to that, as he created one of the most iconic brands: Virgin. Consider Earl Nightingale, a self-development teacher with one of the most distinctive voices. Or what about Usain Bolt? With a name like "Bolt" he couldn't be anything but the fastest man alive. There's MAGIC in names you can tap into... and you get to create the meaning that serves your bigger story. For me, it's an amazing wink from the Universe that my birthday is 9-25 and inside sterling silver you'll see .925 stamped on it.

EXPLORE YOUR NAME

Uh huh...

Are You Wearing Purple Glasses?

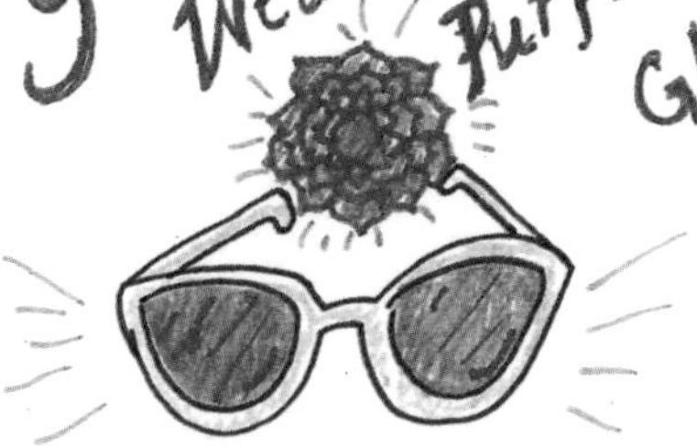

That's what I ask my kids. I wanted to explain how our judgements, filters and pre-set attitude impact what we see and how we respond. I would ask my son, Zack, if one of his friends did what Zoe, his sister, did to him, would he react the same way? Of course, the answer is "No." But wearing purple glasses makes everything look like it has a purple tint to them, an annoyance beyond what happens when others would do something to them. We pass everything through our own filters and beliefs, attempting to make it line up with what we expect to see or have happen. Try changing someone's mind about a deeply held political or religious idea- it won't happen. Everything that fits their worldview looks "purple." But then I thought: why should purple glasses be about a bias that doesn't serve us? What if the purple lenses were about the preconceived idea of a grand cosmic destiny unfolding before your eyes? Everything you see happening is actually happening for your highest evolutionary growth. Every meeting, book, resource, ally & event is there for you! Every so-called obstacle or setback moves more and more in alignment with your true path that is shown in purple. These are much better than rose-colored glasses... purple reveals your cosmic blueprint unfolding perfectly... Perfectly Purple

[Purple is associated with supernatural energy and the cosmos because it is the closest visible wavelength of electromagnetic energy, a few steps from x-rays and gamma rays.]

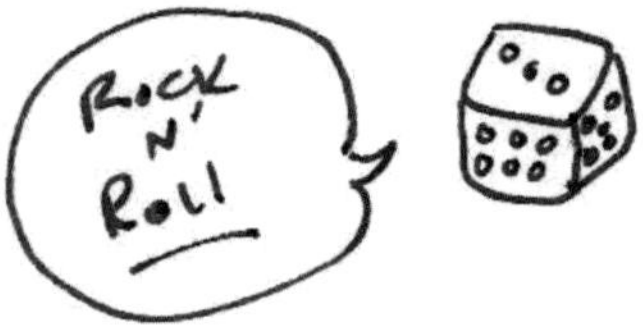
ROCK N' ROLL

YOU ARE NOW IN KNOWING

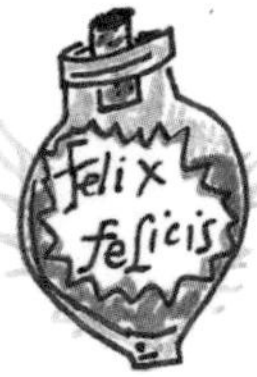

Felix
Felicis

Now is the only time you have to
give you guidance. Imagine having the
Felix Felicis potion from Harry Potter –
This "good luck" potion was really just about
being fully present and moving in full alignment.
Beyond intuition even... You are now in knowing
you have the entire galactic library at your side...
the knowing of the path illuminated by your heart. Simply
being here full of awe, grace and pure ease. When you
pick a path out of alignment, you know it. That's
when your intuition and gut say, "I told you so."
That's your calibration system and that's how the
guardrails are in place moving you towards your full
evolutionary growth. But you can keep yourself from
bumping those edges by ((simply knowing you are guided)).
Your destination is already reserved – and you have
one of 7 billion unique ways back to the ONE.
It's always in the right direction and right timing...
but many times it's the road less taken. It's not the
"safe" and "secure" way because there is little growth
from the same route. Source wants to provide you
with the "good luck" you have available ALL the time.
It's with trust, faith and full surrender to something
bigger than the "small" you. This journal is your path to being
fully supported... It's for you and also those awakening with you.

@: What's the Universe Saying
To You Right Now?

_____

_____

_____

_____

_____

Now make it fit This acronym:

G. _____ @:

R. _____

A. _____

C. _____

E. _____

Whatever the question is...

ONLY

NOW

IS THE ANSWER

Imagination is one of our greatest gifts to create. However, our imagination creates more suffering than we need to experience when applied to the past and the future. Regret is imagining what we did "wrong" in the past and what we wish we could change. Sometimes (actually most of the time) it's the "story" we made up of what happened. One of my friends told me he spent a whole weekend worried he offended me about a post he made that I may have believed he was talking about me. I didn't think that, but he only found out by checking in with me. If regret is being stuck in the past, our imagination can also be engaged in the future of "what if?" The anxiety of considering what could go wrong or catastrophe may befall you. Unless you consider that, you'll be blindsided, right? Hedging your joy and happiness in the moment because something could happen. The worry of tomorrow sucks the life out of today. But it's not just a negative future, you can also be so focused on what things will look like when they're perfect, that you never appreciate HERE. WE ONLY HAVE NOW...

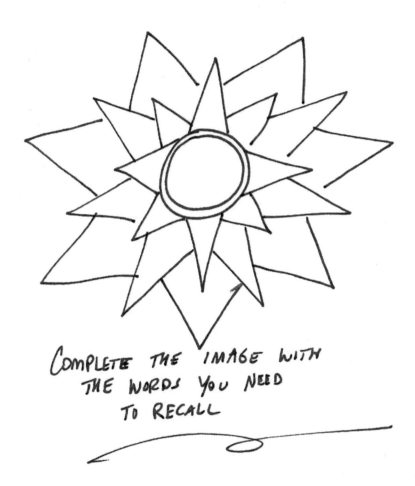

COMPLETE THE IMAGE WITH
THE WORDS YOU NEED
TO RECALL

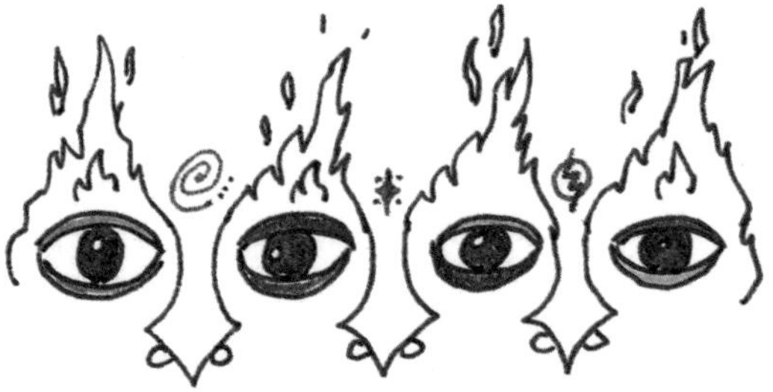

See

WITH YOUR SOUL'S EYES

Your Greatest Vision will never be seen by taking what is currently seen... you need to look within. Seeing the future with the alignment of head, heart and highest purpose. Let spirit give you the kaleidoscopic sight of a brighter future for all.

Train yourself to look beyond your physical eyes. When you meet someone, can you see WHO they really are, beyond appearances? Can you look at a situation beyond what it seems is here?

Your gift is opening up to sight beyond seeing.

LOOK BEYOND

See your true soul path...
See your true soul plan...
See your true soul purpose...

"Close both eyes to see with the other eye"
— RUMI

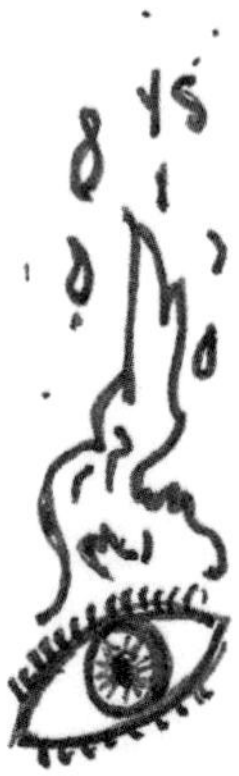

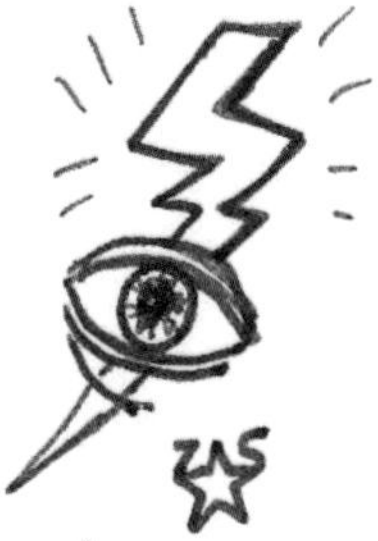
ZAS

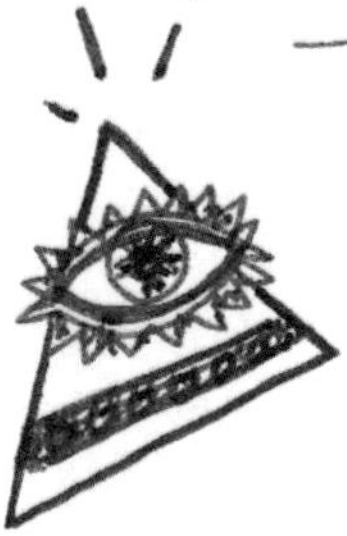

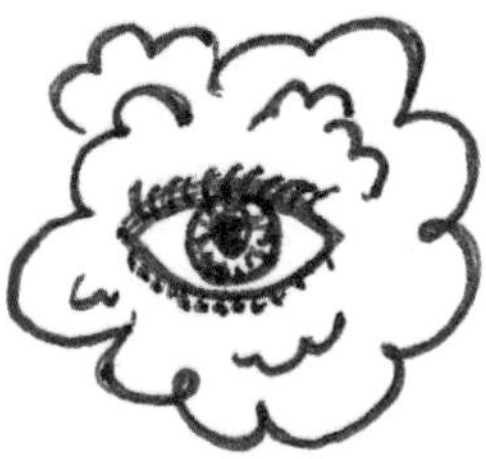

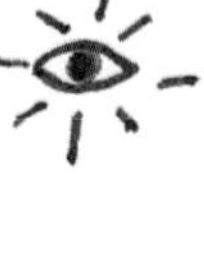

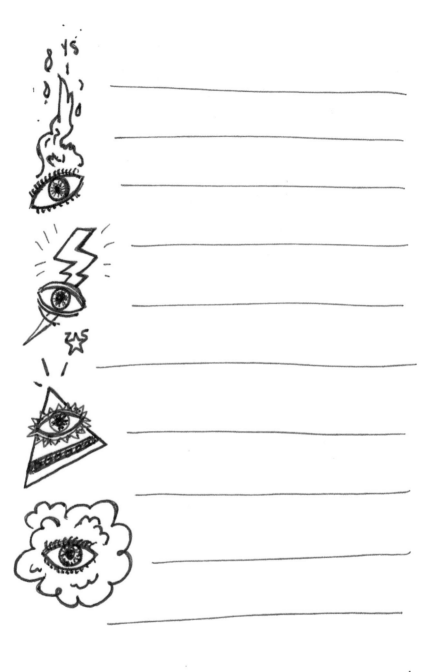

I SEE YOU...

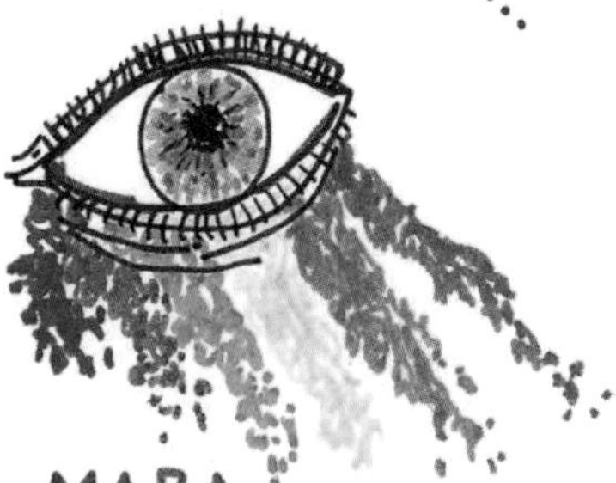

MARA

There is an often told story of the night before Buddha's enlightenment, he fought a great battle against Mara, the demon god. Mara attempted everything he could from the emotions of lust, greed, anger, uncertainty and more. But the would-be Buddha didn't give in - he achieved enlightenment. However Mara was not giving up. Mara would still come but instead of ignoring or fighting him, the Buddha would peacefully bring awareness to the presence, simply saying, "I see you, Mara." And then invite him to tea as a guest. They would sit together for some time, and then Mara would leave and the Buddha remained at ease.

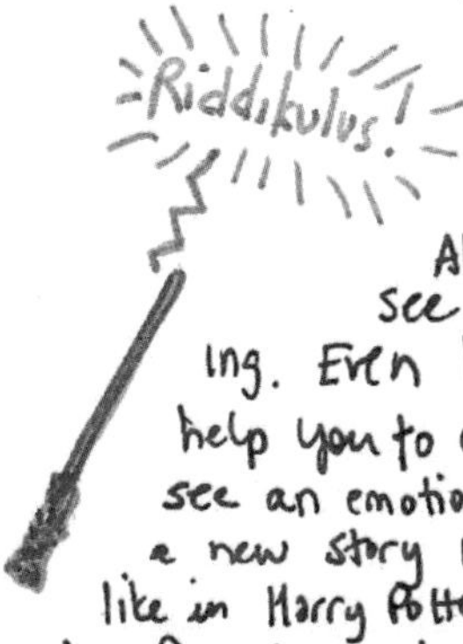
Riddikulus!

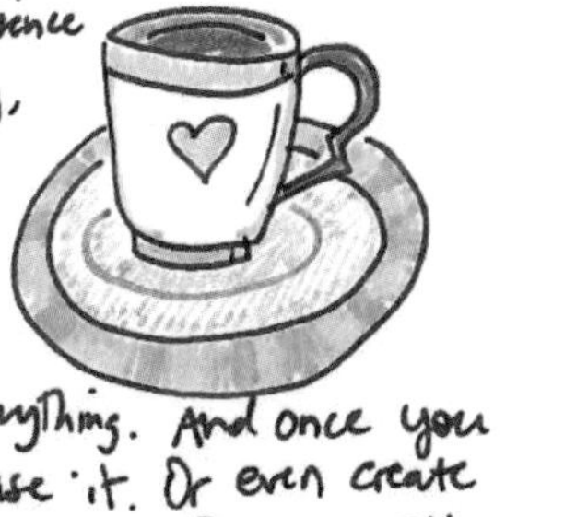

Anytime you experience fear, pain or worry, you too can meet it. Aknowledge the guest and see the "gift" it is bringing. Even bringing awareness can help you to open your heart to everything. And once you see an emotion fully, you can release it. Or even create a new story with more meaning or lightness for you. It's like in Harry Potter where the spell "Riddikulus!" was used to transform boggarts into something funny. The boggarts would assume the shape of the thing we most feared and dreaded. What we hide from or push away only grows in strength and holds power over us. You cannot out-power these teachers - you simply allow, observe and let go...

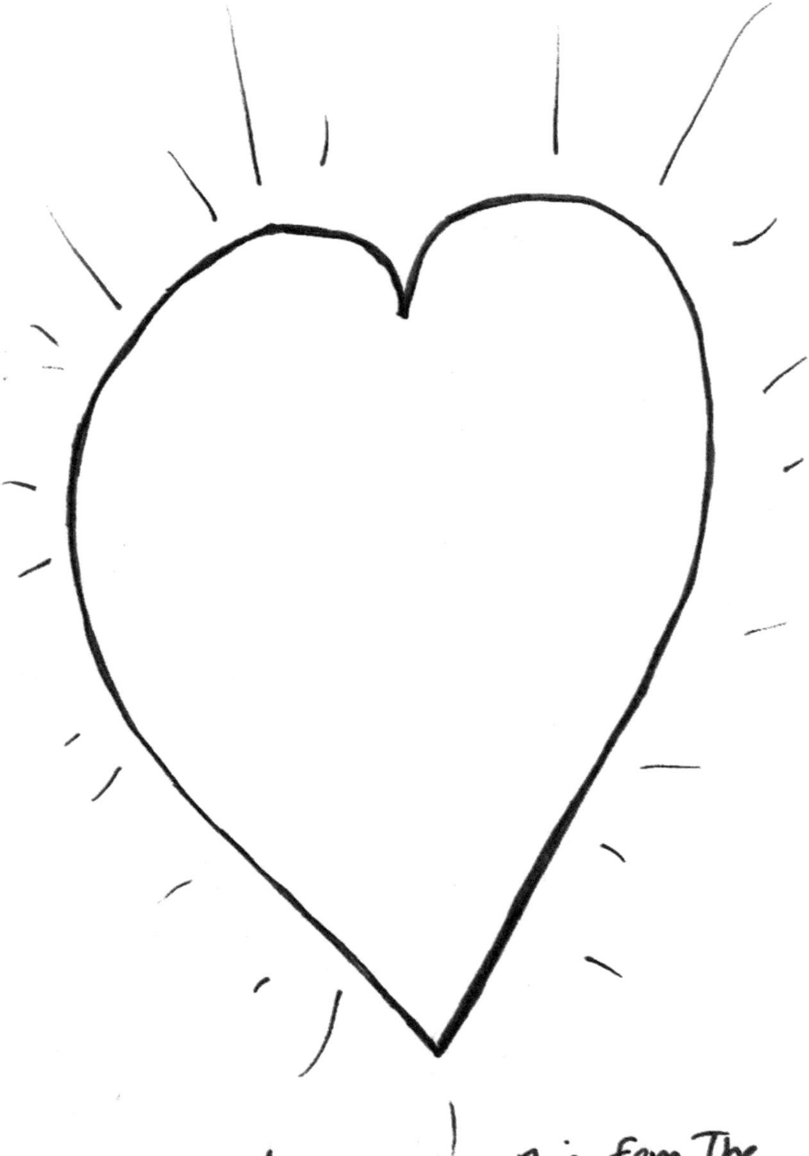

How would you apply this from the greatest expression of LOVE?

HEART OPEN

YOU CAN NEVER CHANGE YOUR SPOTS...

BECAUSE YOUR SPOTS OF SOUL NEVER CHANGE

Anything That can change is <u>NOT</u> real – Therefore what doesn't change is our **soul**. The real spots...

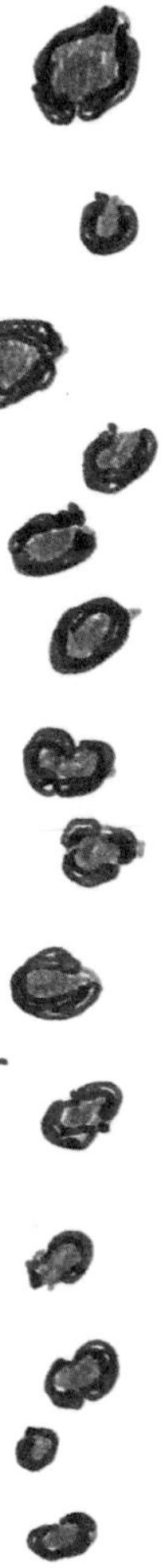

It's about lifting off The coverings of fear, blanket of ego, coating of smallness and layer of undeservedness.

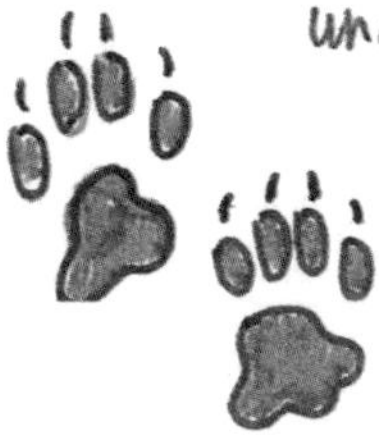

It's RE-remembering WHO you actually are.

Your spots are spots of locations, symbols + ART to see Through the illusion of what changes and what remains.

Yes, you are always evolving but your true self, The soul, does not change. Those spots remain in <u>the perfect pattern, only coming into focus as you recognize yourself again... for the "first" time.</u>

To return to seeing each and every Spot as your roadmap here.

Each is The unique expression of Your true path + essence... but also part of The ultimate <u>Spot</u>light of consciousness illuminating.

Wherever you are right now This is your...

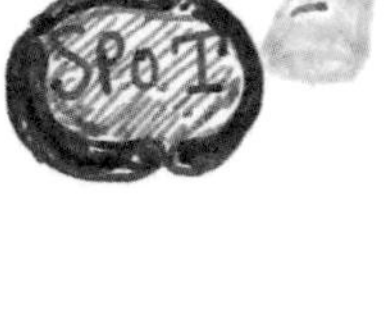
SPOT

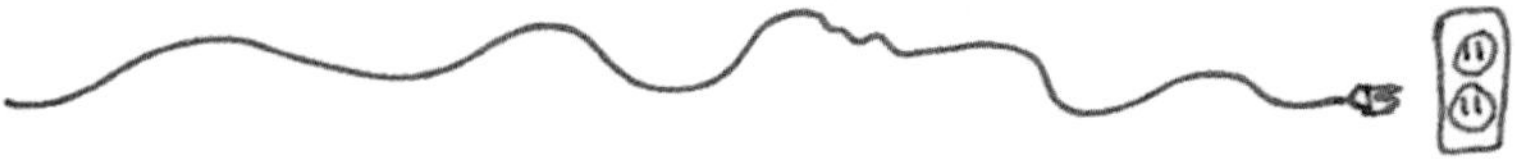

FOUR

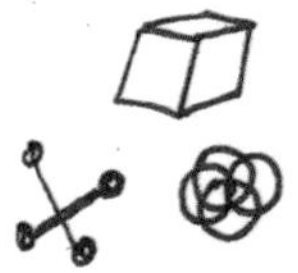

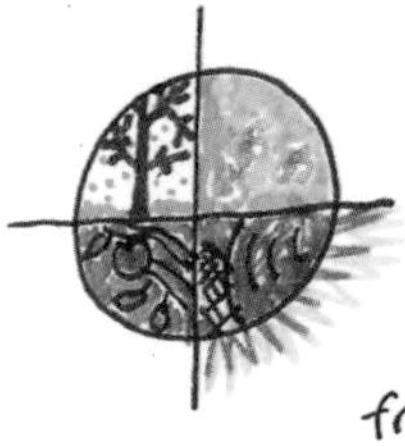

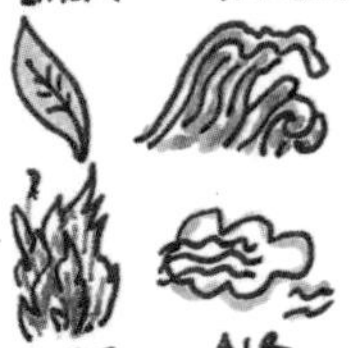
EARTH
WATER
FIRE
AIR

Four is the number of the ancient elements and cycles.
One of the earliest personality profiles involves predicting how we act based on how much we have of each element within us + how we express those characteristics. We're all "made" of the same elements, after all. You can probably think of friends and colleagues who are more fiery than others, or those who flow naturally, or others grounded like the earth. It's easy to dismiss the ancients as clumsy in their application of these 4 elements – but there is something to deep wisdom like this passed through the ages. Taken together with the intelligence of the seasons, you have a way to look at the world + be in harmony with the CYCLES

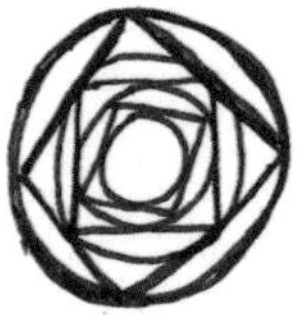

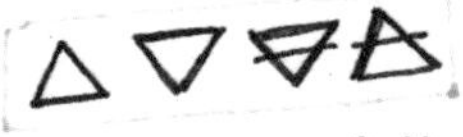

Imagine your life as a macrocosm of the four seasons. Spring is your birth (or rebirth); Summer is growth and advancement. Fall is the time of harvest, when you discover how to gather your strength and lessons. Then winter is the time of retreat, before moving into the ultimate next cycle on the other side.

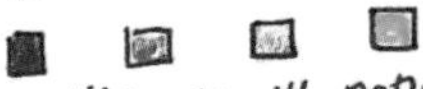

Pay attention to your own life - you'll notice cycles within cycles. You'll definitely notice in your business. "Spring" is the time of creativity and new ideas; the energy is high and passionate. "Summer" is the growth of these ideas and "fall" is the harvest; you have a high reputation, your brand is built-up, etc. And then "winter," if we harvested consciously, we will bloom again in a different way and re-invent ourselves. The cycles for innovation, disruption and breakthroughs are shorter + shorter - everything is accelerating - but that doesn't mean we are able to escape the natural cycles + rhythms of nature. So many times we want to push and push - but the timing might not be correct.
Are you truly in FLOW?

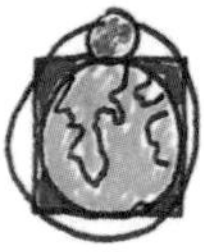

Will power only works until it doesn't. It's much easier when you are working in harmony with your right SEASON.

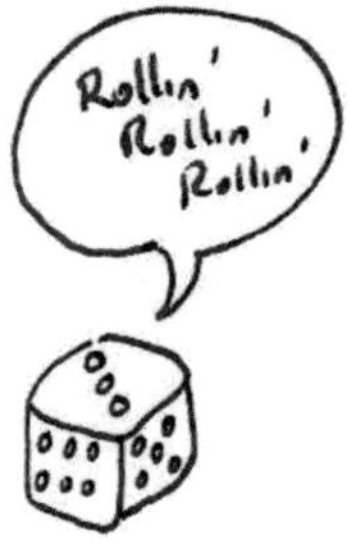
Rollin'
Rollin'
Rollin'

Let THE SEEDS YOU ARE PLANTING Grow!

Allow the seeds to grow - you constantly pull up the roots and expect a mighty oak to thrive...

Your seeds of Intention have already been planted, watered and nourished. It's now time to allow them to continue blossoming. Have your joy, full heart and (business) mind to converse together.

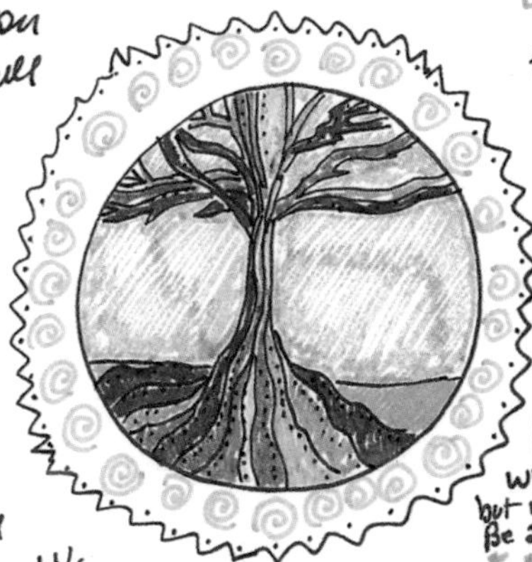

INSTRUCTIONS:

STEP 1: "Thank You" - Magic begins with specifically stating + writing what you are grateful for

STEP 2: "Do I Really Want This?" Like really-really? With my full ♥ Not just nice to have But full alignment

STEP 3: Write - Write your intentions. Write what you want to see, places to go, people to meet. BIG things + small things.

STEP 4: BE AWARE + LET GO What you wrote is headed to you, but you also take action to MEET it. Be awake for signs + symbols.

YOU ARE IN A PLACE - of - DIVINE TIMING & INTERSECTION

You've already done the 'work' in your journal, in your concepts, ideas, your relationships, network, skills + lessons. The pins are stacked

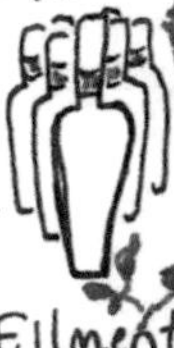

Allow yourself to ASK for and receive your full abundance of creation + fulfillment

_____

_____

_____

_____

_____

_____

_____

_____

_____

_____

The Right SEEDS Always Bloom ...

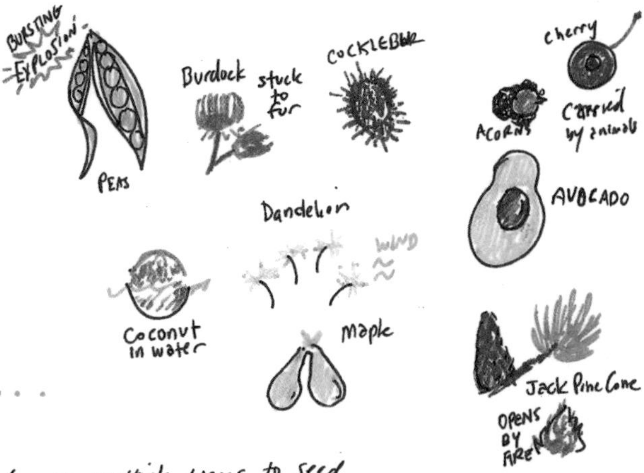

PEAS — BURSTING EXPLOSION

Burdock stuck to fur

COCKLEBUR

cherry — Carried by animals

ACORNS

AVOCADO

Dandelion — WIND

Coconut in water

maple

Jack Pine Cone — OPENS BY FIRE

Nature has figured out multiple ways to seed the Earth. Some seeds are covered in an appealing and sweet casing like the cherry. That's pretty smart since animals + humans are drawn to eat it, and then like a Trojan horse the seed gets deposited somewhere else. A plant is smart enough to know its progeny may have more success some distance away. As parents, we can pay attention here to ensure our seedlings don't grow up in our shadows. Our children need their own soil to bloom fully.

Seeds are designed to be abundant and adaptive

Some are spread on the wind like the "helicopter" maple seeds I loved watching rain down around me when I was a kid. Or other seeds, like the cocklebur, hitch a free ride in animals' fur. The coconut is uniquely designed to float in the water for long periods of time, protecting the precious cargo inside until it makes its way onshore. And there are even seeds that lay dormant until a fire comes and razes the ground around them. These seeds sprout from destruction to bring new life! The symbolism here is not subtle.

What Seeds Are You Planting?
(AKA IDEAS)

How many different ways can your ideas spread? Can you create incentives (the fruit) that attract others to help you? Or what ideas can hitch a ride by fast movers and influencers? Some ideas might sprout after destruction — rising from the ashes of "failure." Perhaps, like the plants, we don't need to be attached to which ideas take root. The right seeds will always bloom when we provide the "water" and "sunlight."

YOU are GALACTIC SEED BLOOMING

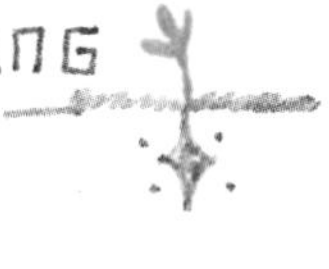

You HAVE EXACTLY <u>18</u> words
to tell yourself about This topic...

————— ————— —————

————— ————— —————

————— ————— —————

————— ————— —————

————— ————— —————

————— ————— —————

Now write an intention or sentence that
contains your insight...

_____

_____

_____

Ein Baum umspannt den Globus

The Name of the Wind

I cast my voice over the wind to claim my Galactic heritage. To fully RE-Remember my mission on Earth. I AM GALACTIC seed blooming.

I AM a COSMIC✳CATALYST.
The wind is my inspiration from the divine. I send out my deepest longing as an infinite Ripple across the cosmos... merging with my deepest essence of perfection & grace... of ØNE.

What other assurances do you need?
You are whole... you are perfect... you are Love shown in the Seasons, the cycles, divine appointments and cosmic appointments. In the moon & the sun + stars That guide home - like the dawning of a new day.

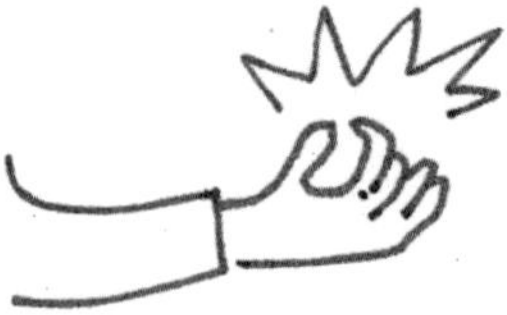

MEDITATE for 8 Minutes

Now What?

We ARE MADE of STAR STUFF...

But Born of the EARTH ⊕

The elements that make up our bodies - and nearly everything else around us - come from out in the Cosmos. Billions and billions of years back, we can trace our origins to stars exploding!

You are literally dust & ashes... but stardust and galactic ashes!

There is a deep longing to return to the stars, but we are already here on our piece of cosmic real estate. We are born of the Earth and also intertwined with our mother. Everything is birthed of the Earth and the cosmic union of stars + galaxies. We are the merging of the two.

That means we contain the full library of the Universe - but also a reason for being part of this world. We are literally tied to it as we experience disorientation not having the Earth's geomagnetic properties regularly.

Perhaps you are here to walk together with your Cosmic Earth siblings to finally help us all graduate to the next stage. Our GALACTIC emergence & Ascension predicted by so many cultures and mythologies. But it starts with ONE. You. The entire Universe is holographic and what we do to evolve ourselves... evolves the cosmic story. It's happening regardless as the Universe's Great Year is birthed... we are given the opportunity to consciously co-create.

Conversation With Your
COSMIC SELF

·✧·

You: Why is This page important to me right now?

@: _____

_____

_____

You: What else should I know?

✧: _____

_____

_____

_____

You: _____

♡ _____

_____

_____

You: What should I call you?

@: _____

XoXo

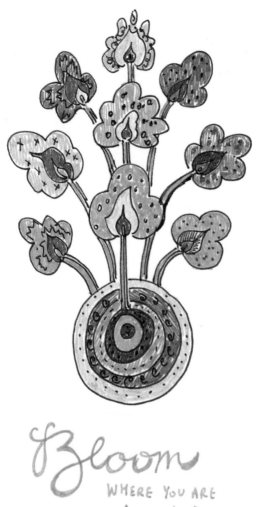

Bloom
WHERE YOU ARE
planet(ed)

As a multi-dimensional being, it might seem difficult to be on Earth during these accelerated times of learning. We long for our place in the stars... but you were brought to Earth for a definite reason in this coming silver age.

Bloom here and embrace being part of + birthed by the Earth. Literally "grown" from this planet... for the collective evolution. Rise to the full merging of your personal self, higher self + divine source. Step forth with everything you've "learned" in the exact spot you are 'planted' or 'plant(ed)'

Why?

Why does this page matter to you right now?

(Whatever you answer, keep asking WHY to get deeper and deeper to the real WHY.)

ANSWER #1: _____

_____

_____

Why? _____

_____

_____

Why? _____

_____

_____

Why? _____

_____

_____

Why? _____

_____

_____

Why? _____

_____

FIVE

Five is the number of biological life and beauty. The planet Venus creates a beautiful five-fold pattern with our home. And five is seen in seeds, flowers, stars – balancing the '3' & '2.' humans have five fingers and toes, plus five senses, so five is a distinct human number – but also linked to our cosmic origin. Why else would we be able to create a 'STAR' with our arms and legs out, in perfect geometry.

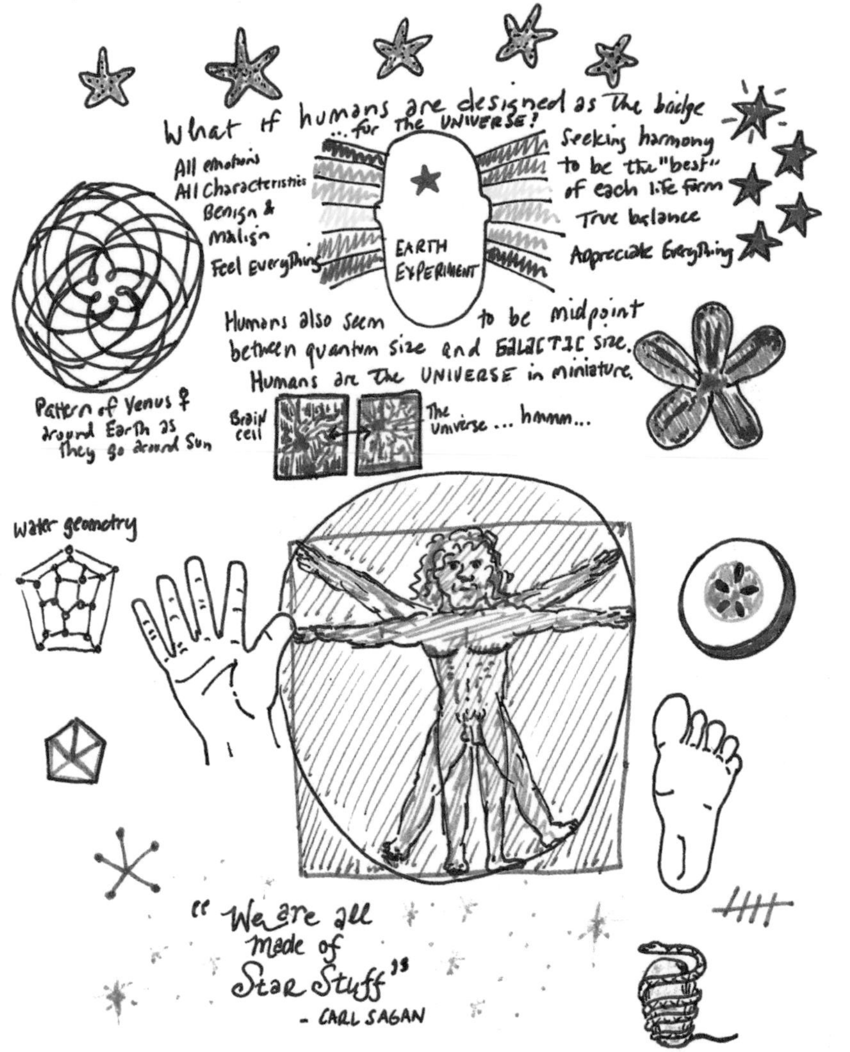
What if humans are designed as the bridge ... for the UNIVERSE?
All emotions
All Characteristics
Benign & Malign
Feel Everything
EARTH EXPERIMENT
Seeking harmony to be the "best" of each life form
True balance
Appreciate Everything
Pattern of Venus ♀ around Earth as they go around Sun
Humans also seem to be midpoint between quantum size and GALACTIC size.
Humans are the UNIVERSE in miniature.
Brain cell
The Universe ... hmmm...
water geometry
"We are all made of Star Stuff"
- CARL SAGAN

 5 Wishes for Yourself

 I AM _____

 I AM _____

 I AM _____

 I AM

 I wish for _____ (unlimited wishes)

Signed: _____
Date: _____

In Gay Hendricks's poignant book, *5 wishes*, he provides the simple (yet powerful) way of ensuring your life was a total success. Here are my 5...

5 WISHES

BY GAY HENDRICKS

1 My life is a total success because I am completely and fully engaged in projects that serve the Global Goals and create joyful abundance for all involved.

2 My life is a total success because I am creating and putting out my GREATEST work through my writing, ART & ideas.

3 My life is a total success because I am now feeling fully, my heart is full, and I am fully present, connected, laughing, having fun & following joy as my GPS.

4 My life is a total success because I am catalyzing the catalysts to the NEXT evolutionary consciousness shift of the SILVER AGE.

5 My life is a total success because I am deeply aligned with synchronicities, signs and symbols across the Universe "talking" to me.

As we live our lives following our deepest intentions, we can never have regret. Answering this question gives you the touchstone and guideposts for everything and anything through all your years forever.

SET A TIMER
AND WRITE NON-STOP
for 6 minutes
(no editing + keep your pen moving)

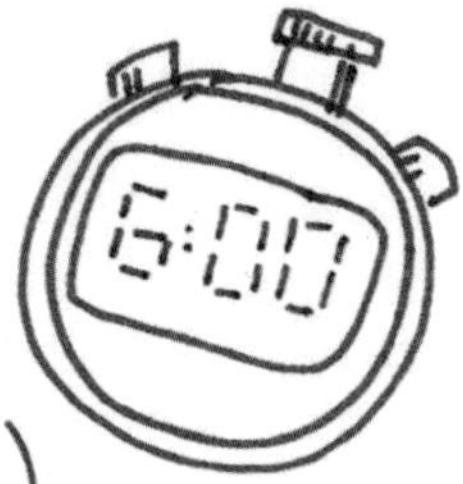
6:00

Okay Go

Keep Going

I AM ___
(insert your choice here)

Those two little words – I AM. Truly powerful because anything that follows is our self pronouncement. You can tell so much about someone by listening to their language. Pay attention to what you say to yourself "I'm tired," or "I AM NOT going to be able to ___." Simply having awareness of what follows "I AM" makes you again the author of your own book. Wayne Dyer talks a lot about "I AM" and the story of Moses seeing the burning bush that would not be consumed. And after an astonishing conversation Moses is given the name he can share, "I AM THAT I AM."

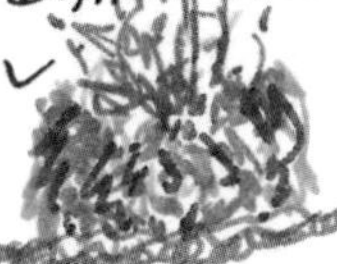

In meditation I very often say my own "I AM" statements. Some of mine include:

- I AM Boundless Love
- I AM Optimal Health
- I AM Joyful Abundance
- I AM THE MAGICAL CHILD
- I AM COSMIC CATALYST

And as I say them I also feel into them. How optimal health feels with energy + zip, my body working properly, feeling light... Or The Magical Child.. I lean into my inner playfulness + smile.* Getting that feeling with the words I AM gives it more energy! The best part is whatever you want you can insert as your choice after those 2 simple words... And you can always change it anytime. Every moment is a good time to ~~rewrite~~ BE your version to match the one.

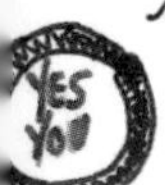
YES
YOU

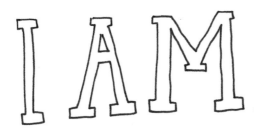

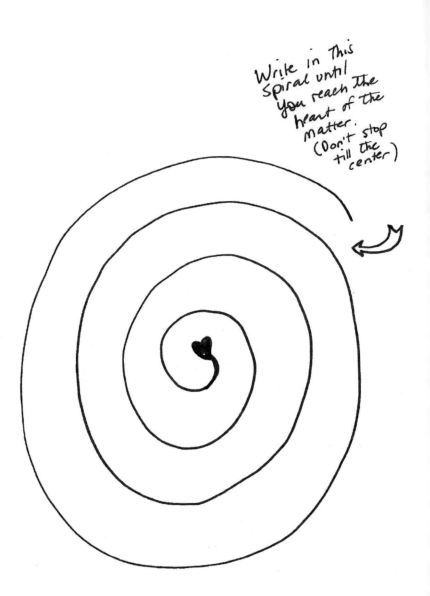

Write in This Spiral until you reach The heart of the matter. (Don't stop till the center)

The World's Greatest Paradox...

WHATEVER Serves the GREATER COLLECTIVE is the MOST SELFISH GIFT You CAN GIVE to Yourself

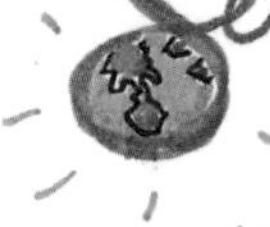

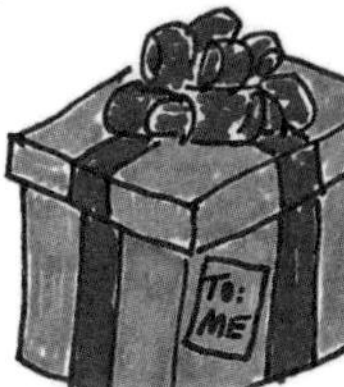
TO: ME

In my earliest journals, I created a value-system for myself. And one of the key statements was...

"I get rich by enriching others **10x - 100x** for what they pay in return"

· Be The One Who Shines For Others.

I was always thinking about how to provide more value because I knew I'd be compensated in multiples of that. It's a great question to ask when selling anything. Also, "How can I ensure I provide 10x - 100x in value here?" Many times that may mean working with partners or joint ventures who can piggyback on what you are providing or considering what to add. There's something hard-wired into humans that we feel good when we help others. Even small acts of kindness trigger this. But even greater is how can entrepreneurs expand this notion to serve bigger numbers? As my colleague Peter Diamandis, founder of X-Prize, likes to say, "Want to become a billionaire? Then help a billion people."

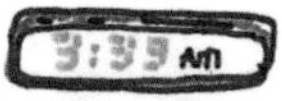
3:33 AM

At exactly 3:33 AM the other night, I woke up from a deep sleep with this download:

"Our greatest gift is our being of service. The more people we help/serve/better - the more selfish it is for us."

And that greatest service is The Evolved Enterprise that makes the greatest impact for the greatest number of customers, team members and all of us on the planet.

YOU ALREADY KNOW THE ANSWER

(But humor me + write it here)

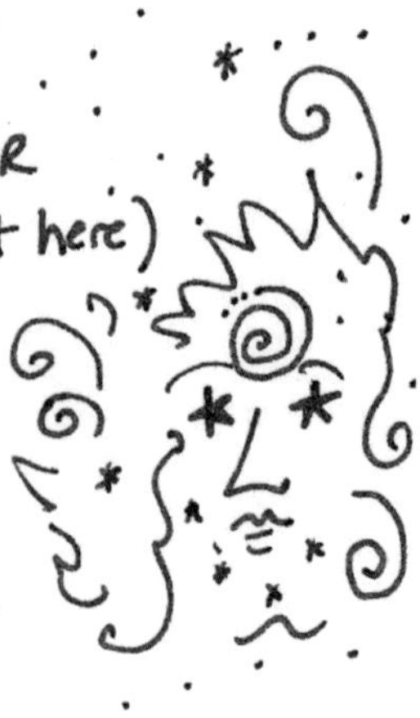

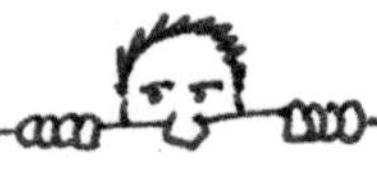

Inspiration:
The Great Wave
off Kanagawa
by Hokusai

YOUR GREAT WAVE
AWAITS

What is your (next) greatest purpose you've scared to proclaim? Your great wave is awaiting your greatest service to the collective. Allow the universe to conspire to help you be the channel for what really matters most.

No question, it's something that might seem too lofty or not in your realm of knowing - but that's not up to you. Your role is to become that channel to see what wants to come through you. To allow the greatest wave of cosmic proportions to take you in service of the evolutionary whole. WHY DID YOU COME HERE?

Set your highest intention + hold on for the ride!

DRAW WHAT YOU FEEL NOW

(Don't worry-nobody is judging)

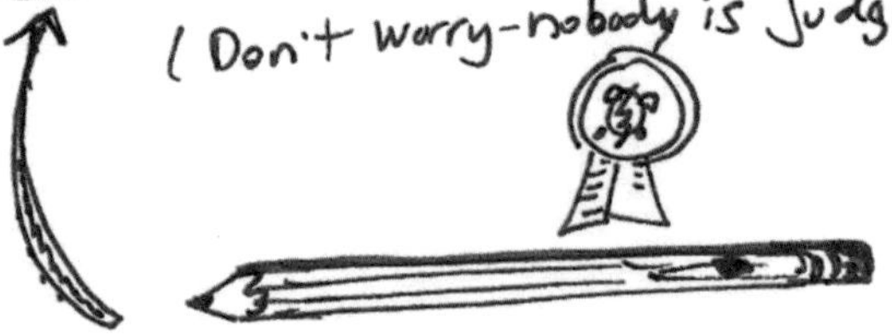

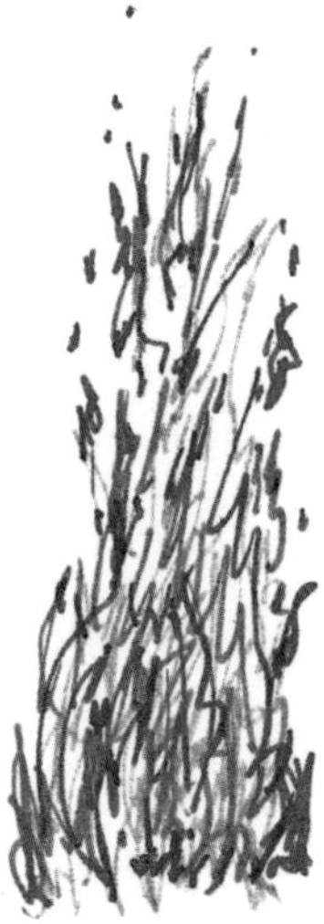

Evoke The Power of the Silver Violet FLAME

There is a stirring... an awakening that cannot be denied... a mythic CALL of some long-felt knowing. Once the Cosmic Alarm Clock has gone off, there really is no turning back on this adventurer's quest. Yes, it's this knowing of being a global—even a Cosmic-Changemaker that is real. It plays out in your mythic storyline of expanded consciousness and evolution. You are required to bring together all your skills, resources, tools, talents, relationships and knowledge into your own ultimate form of artistry. Your personal experience is holographic and empowers galactic ascension. You cannot have written within you a deep desire to answer this clarion call without also having the seed blueprinted within you to bloom by Universal Source.

Call to your allies of joyful abundance. The magical inner child, your spirit totem and guardians & guides for your complete RE-Remembering. Fulfill your DESTINY...

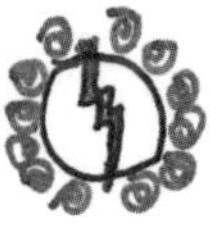

CONNECT
—
CATALYZE
—
CO-CREATE

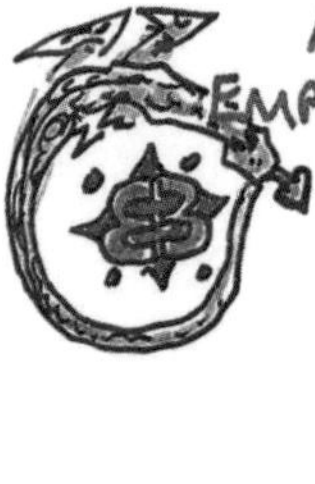

AWAKEN YOUR SOUL...
EMPOWER the GLOBAL VISIONARIES

_____

_____

_____

_____

_____

_____

_____

_____

_____

_____

_____

SIX

Six is known as The PERFECT number of structure, creation and order. From Genesis the world was made in 6 days to highlight this property. Mathematically the factors of 6 are 1, 2 + 3.

$$1 + 2 + 3 = \boxed{6}$$

Not just their sum either... $1 \times 2 \times 3 = \boxed{6}$

Each snowflake has its own intricate design, yet all follow the perfect hexagonal pattern. In the same way, each human is a beautiful expression of the same pattern. Two snowflakes might form in the exact same cloud, but their distinct journeys down will produce unique shapes. Even identical twins, formed from the same DNA, will have unique individual characteristics based on their experiences, thoughts and influences.

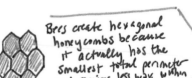

The "seed" of life is known as the blueprint for the next expansion of the "Flower of Life" containing creation.

Bees create hexagonal honeycombs because it actually has the smallest total perimeter and requires less wax within a given volume

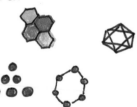

You've been given your own perfect structure for your growth and development — what will You do with it? No matter what, it will still be perfect. How can it not be? Even if it doesn't seem like it at the moment — but set inside The cosmic Mosaic, the crystaline structure is in divine order. There can be no mistake, no regrets, no wrong ways of doing here and now. Rejoice! There are over 7 billion unique expressions of perfection all converging into one. The structure is holographically expansive and then merges back into oneness with new information from your experience and journey. Thank You!

You HAVE EXACTLY __18__ Words
to tell yourself about This topic...

____ ____ ____

____ ____ ____

____ ____ ____

____ ____ ____

____ ____ ____

____ ____ ____

Now write an intention or Sentence that
contains your insight...

_____

_____

_____

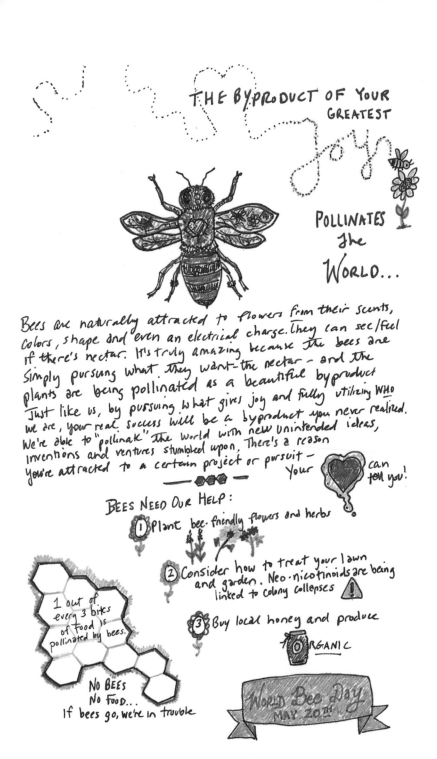

THE BYPRODUCT OF YOUR GREATEST joy POLLINATES the WORLD...

Bees are naturally attracted to flowers from their scents, colors, shape and even an electrical charge. They can see/feel if there's nectar. It's truly amazing because the bees are simply pursuing what they want - the nectar - and the plants are being pollinated as a beautiful byproduct. Just like us, by pursuing what gives joy and fully utilizing WHO we are, your real success will be a byproduct you never realized. We're able to "pollinate" the world with new unintended ideas, inventions and ventures stumbled upon. There's a reason you're attracted to a certain project or pursuit — Your ♥ can tell you!

BEES NEED OUR HELP:

① Plant bee-friendly flowers and herbs

② Consider how to treat your lawn and garden. Neo-nicotinoids are being linked to colony collapses ⚠

③ Buy local honey and produce. ORGANIC

1 out of every 3 bites of food is pollinated by bees.

NO BEES NO FOOD... If bees go, we're in trouble

World Bee Day MAY 20th

Roll, Baby, roll...

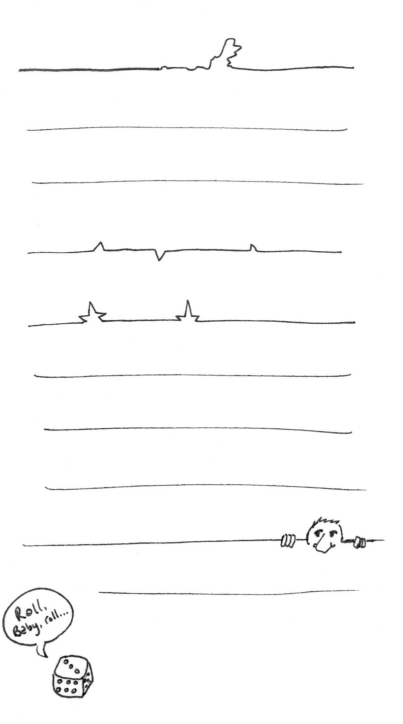

AS ABOVE

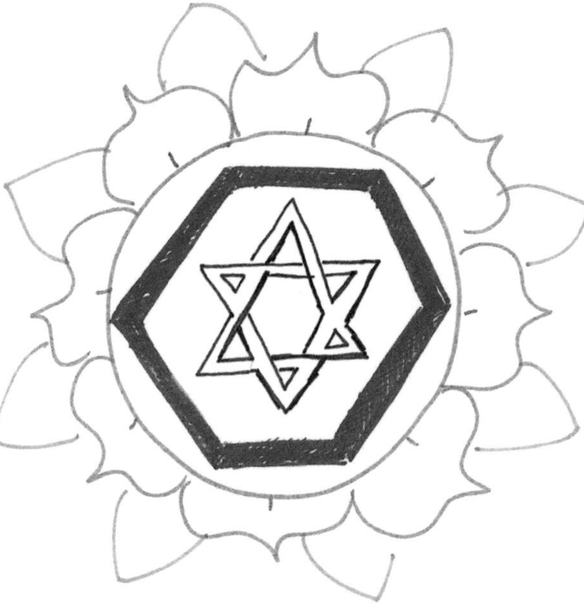

SO BELOW

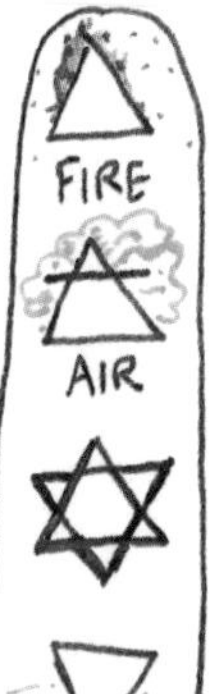
FIRE
AIR
WATER
EARTH

Heaven is here now by bringing our highest self together with our material world.

Our inner world is a mirror and reflection of the outer. It's easy to think "fixing" something here is the secret, but the spirit above is our ruler below.

Re-unite all the elements of WHO you are with the highest realm.

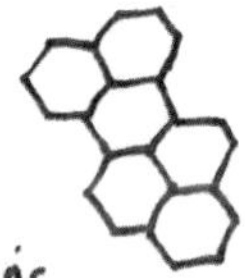

There are two movements: The heavens reaching down and the physical moving back to spirit. The symbolism shows both and represents the Universe's code for how opposites bring creation. And there is quite a bit of MAGIC here too!

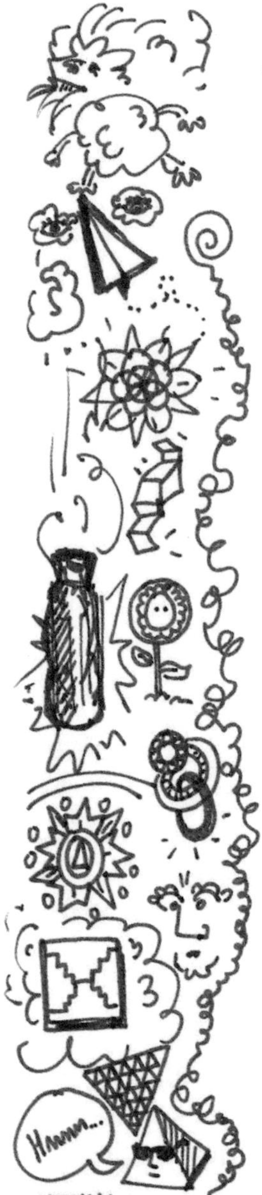
Hmmm...

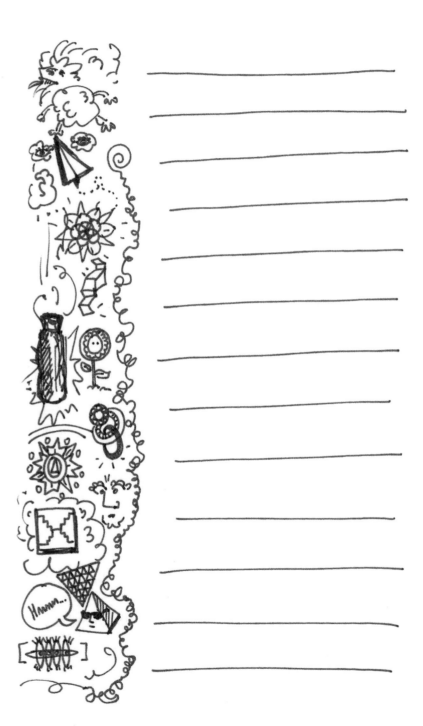

TEACH THE WAY BY LIVING THE WAY

- Meditation & Mindfulness
- Full expression of unique talents
- Continual growth & EXPANSION
- Powerful ACTIVATION of language ("I am ___")
- Gratitude & AWE
- LOVE ♡ WITH A FULL HEART
- Unite the head, heart, highest purpose & happy inner child
- Playfulness
- Intuitive knowing & cheerful expectancy without attachment
- Optimize physical body with nourishment & exercise
- Joyful abundance
- Divine Destiny unfolding in everything
- Catalyze the Cosmos (Light 1,000 Suns!)

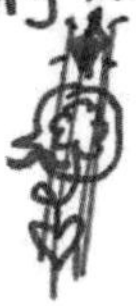

Your actions shout so loudly... That your words only whisper softly...

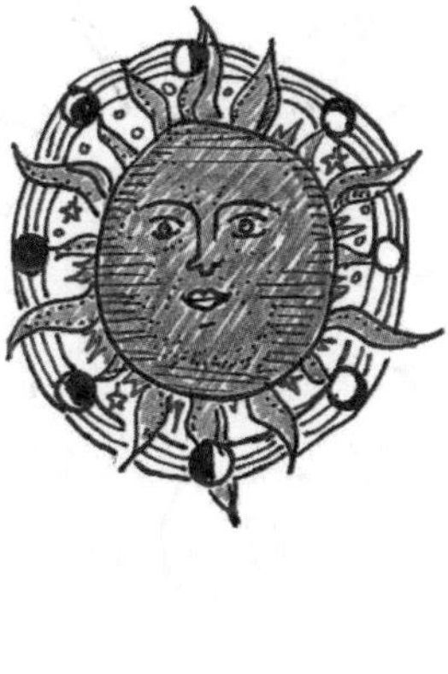

I've only left guideposts for others to live their own teachings
-Y.S.

ZOOM OUT AND
SEE THE BIG PICTURE

Pull back and see everything about This... What
is the bigger story and reason ?

_____

_____

_____

_____

_____

_____

_____

_____

ZOOM OUT & EVERYTHING Changes

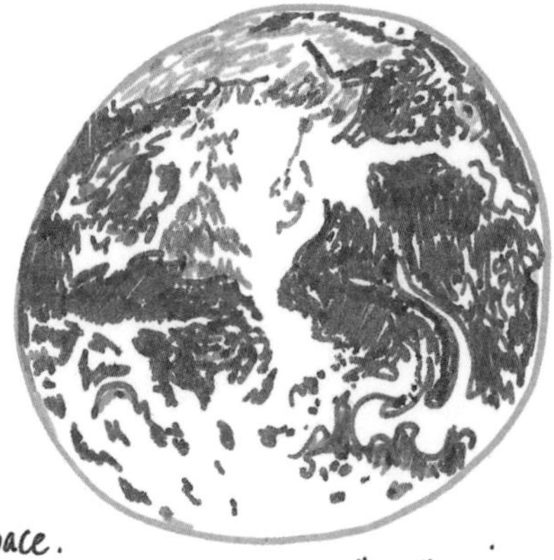

THE OVERVIEW EFFECT IS something astronauts report after viewing the Earth from space.

Everything shifts suddenly. All the "BIG" issues and conflicts below, seem tiny and meaningless. There's an immediate sense of the awe wonder and fragility of life on our blue marble. From that vantage point, there are no man-made country borders artificially dividing us from each other. We are all passengers on Spaceship Earth... hurling through space. ⊕

When you change your perspective to a more elevated view, doesn't your issue or problem shift? How many times have you been consumed by something - maybe even a significant tragedy - but from a later viewpoint, you could actually see the gifts hidden there for you? Or how time heals wounds. Imagine everything we believe is so important at this moment is all going on on a giant rock speeding through space at 1,000 mph!

⊕

"You develop an instant global consciousness, a people orientation, an intense dissatisfaction with the state of the world, and a compulsion to do something about it."

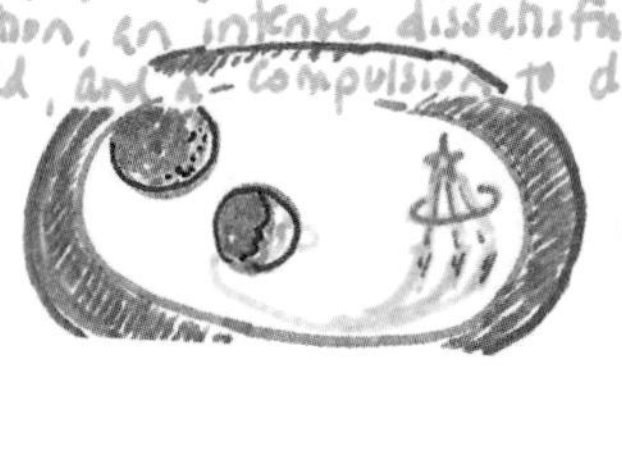

Edgar Mitchell, Apollo 14
(This experience caused Mitchell to co-found the Institute of Noetic Sciences - IONS)

You Already
Know the Answer
(But humor me + write it here)

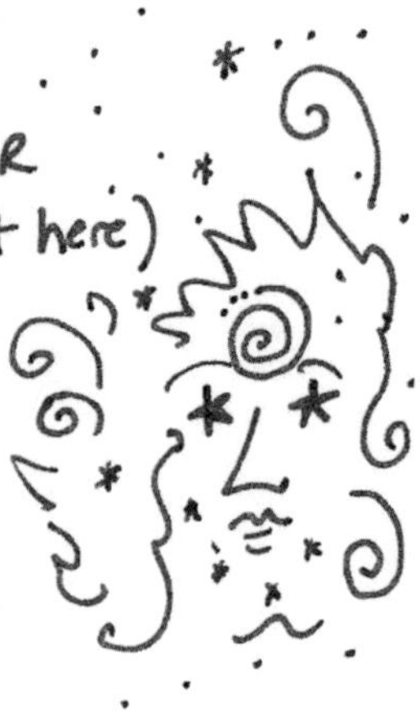

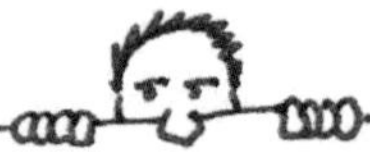

ASSEMBLE · THE · LIGHT · COUNCILS ·

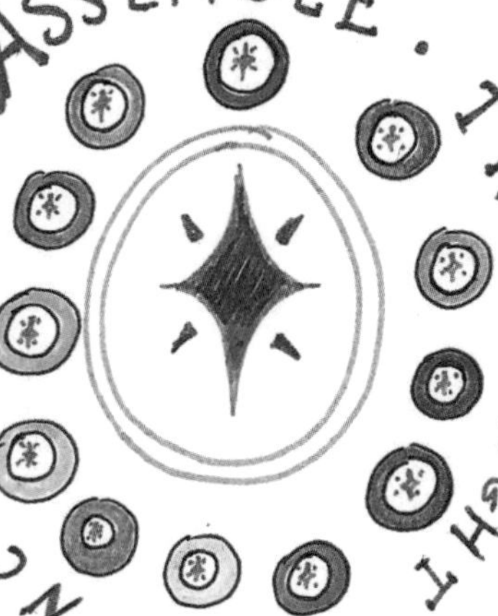

You immediately KNOW when you encounter another who shares a deep destiny with you. No matter the "wrapper," the inside is encoded with an interconnected piece of the puzzle for you. Some people have called this a "soul group" or "soul family." It doesn't matter the name—there is something that clicks. It excites you! Lights you up in their presence!

Perhaps part of your mission here on Earth is to put the "gang" back together! Perhaps you've even shared multiple lifelines together →
And part of the fun is the cosmic hide and seek you each play until the time is just right!

What did you volunteer for here?

... Then these Light Councils merge with other circles ... and those align with other commUNITYies

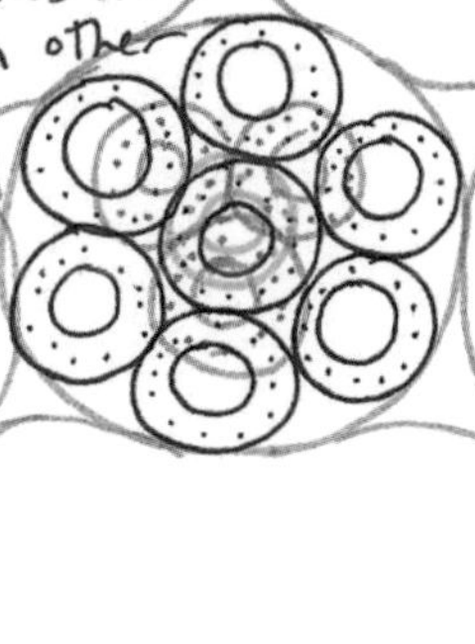

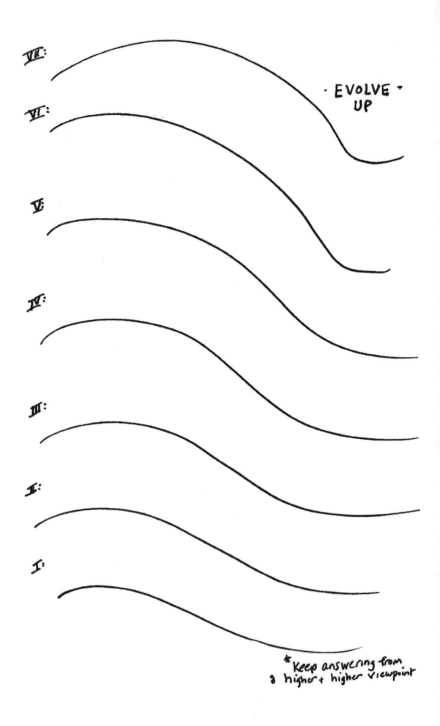

VII:

VI:

· EVOLVE ·
UP

V:

IV:

III:

II:

I:

I:

* Keep answering from
a higher + higher viewpoint

* **THE THRESHOLD:**

Each evolutionary turn, you must give up what you Thought you Are or knew to make the next leap. Surrender into the Divine Mystery.. Sometimes it even feels like a step backwards

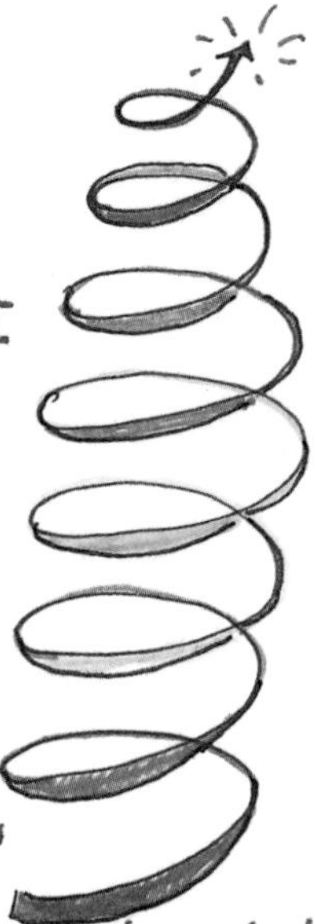

YOUR EVOLUTIONARY PATH IS SIMPLY **INEVITABLE**

You Just choose When & How Fast

The Universe is designed to create more Universe creators. It's absolutely inevitable - you simply decide how "long" you'd like it to take. (That's in Chronos time - in KAIROS time it all happens NOW.)

What's the first Thing humans did when we built a 3D printer? We created a 3-D printer to print more 3-D printers, obviously. The Universe is the same - it wants to teach "you" how to move from a denser place back to light. Your path is assured - and at each revolution and cycle, you decide to graduate or not. Moving from survival and simply pleasing the ego - up through feeling through your heart, sharing your voice and ultimately merging with your highest self... Then moving upward again & again! Up Through the next octave. Part of our path is teaching + opening up to a bigger role. We evolve into having more reach + leverage using conscious intention... how do we quickly move from intention to "reality" That supports and nourishes ALL. That's part of the secret. And Then bringing up others "lower" than us by teaching and stepping into our next higher evolution. Each turn has its own perils - but it gets easier + harder. Harder to give up what came before.* Easier because you know what's coming. The NEXT LEAP! GALACTIC EMERGENCE...

"Sorry, you were designed for This...
Now get on with it..."

What's the First Thing to do?

____

Date completed: ______________

Second Thing:

____

Date completed: ______________

Third:

____

Date Completed: ______________

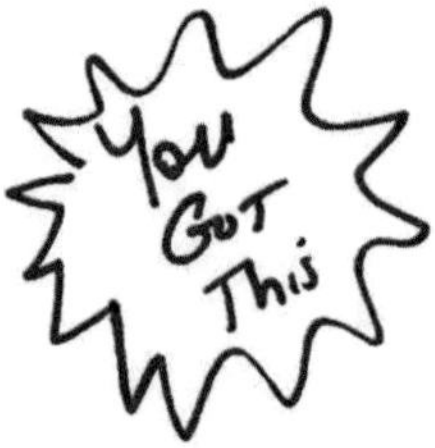
You
Got
This

✦ WANTED ✦

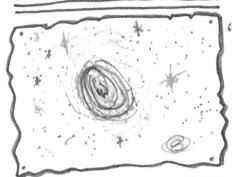

" ... One of the good things about the system is that the system wants to teach you about itself. "
— Itzhak Bentov

UNIVERSE CREATORS

How Does The Universe Think?

If you're an engineer it will teach you in structure, an artist will see in visual flashes. and an entrepreneur gets the message in ecosystem thinking... like interconnected rainforests or coral reefs.

Think about the 3D printer that creates objects on the spot. That's one level of creation, but the next META level is the 3D printer that prints more 3D printers. Nearly everything follows nature's blueprint to create more and more...

Life Simply Wants More Life

Creation Wants More Creation

Leaders shouldn't be praised for how many followers they have, but for how many other leaders they've created. And it's not just creation, but how these creation pieces are a holographic part of the whole, like Russian nesting dolls.

Each piece is simultaneously a whole and a part of the next bigger structure:

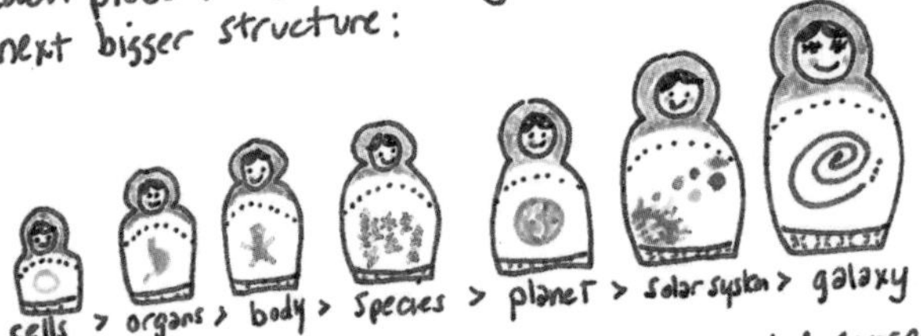

cells > organs > body > species > planet > solar system > galaxy

The Universe is waiting to see who gains an expanded consciousness and then gives you more divine assignments serving the collective.

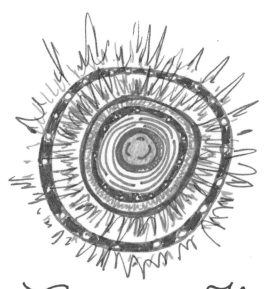

CATALYZE The COSMOS

Light 1,000 suns who can light 1,000 more suns!

"If a thousand suns were to rise
in the heavens at the same time,
the blaze of their light would resemble
the splendor of that Supreme Spirit."
#LIGHT1000SUNS — Bhaghavad Gita

A sun nourishes life everywhere, and together 1000 suns
is a cosmic mosaic enveloping the Universe and beyond.
If they also light 1,000 suns, there are 1,000,000 lights
of splendor ablaze! The radiance and illumination would
alight all the cracks + crevices where darkness lingers still.

Once upon a time...

(What's the REAL story?)

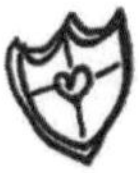

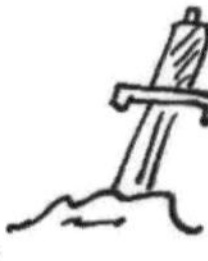

#COSMICJOURNAL

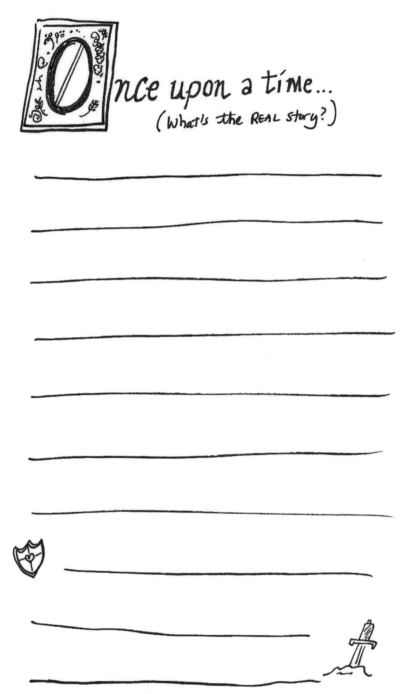

Write the Business Love Story You Want the World to - Buy -

Love is not a 4 letter word in business. In fact, it is _the_ competitive advantage that helps move you from a transactional to transformational company ... and even transcending what business can be. No more business as usual. Allow _your work_ to become _your_ art. The canvas is your Company. When you align the True "soul" of your business with more impact, meaning and happiness - you inevitably create even greater profits ... as an Evolved Enterprise.

🪷

But This cannot happen by doing what you've always done. It requires merging your head, heart and highest purpose. It means following That nagging voice That you have something more to offer. It requires asking the tough questions without easy answers. It means being willing to pursue your greatest vision without full assurance it'll "work." There's a change coming...

((Build the damn Thing already because your perfect customers are waiting to fall in love with you!))

🪷

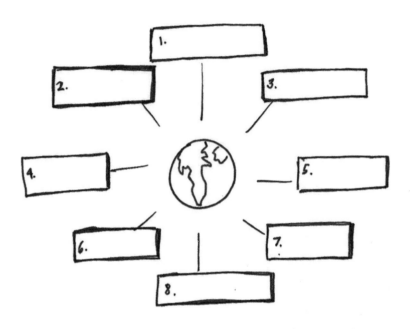

1.

2.

3.

4.

5.

6.

7.

8.

What are the 8 key points here that
will "change" your world?

WHO ARE YOU TO PLAY SMALLER?

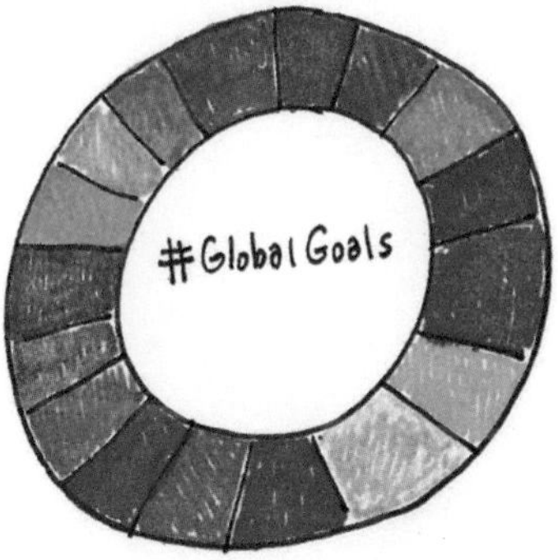
#GlobalGoals

Who does that serve? Not you, not the world. It's a false humble... Your **JOY** is in

FULL SERVICE.

It only requires your full 'effortless effort' to totally embrace and align with your destiny. Not in an ego way but as fulfilling the greatest service to the collective – and the byproducts are immense.

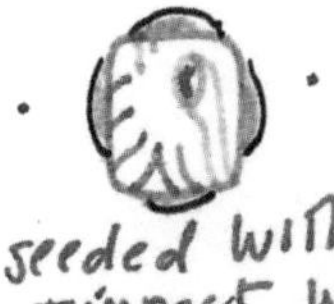

You cannot have seeded within you the vision to make a significant impact without also having the resources, allies and ability to actually accomplish it.

Is this really blank?

WELCOME TO THE ASCENDING...

SILVER AGE

COMING SOON

♫ "WE ARE ON TIME..."
-Nahko + Medicine for the people
#108/108

GOLDEN AGE
SATYA
SILVER
TRETA
TRETA
SILVER
BRONZE
DWAPARA
KALI
DWAPARA
BRONZE
IRON

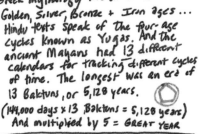

Can you feel what's happening?
There's an acceleration of consciousness...
Mindfulness is just one leading factor. A few years ago, if I asked a room how many meditate, only a small group of hands would go up. Now, it's much larger - sometimes the majority. The number of conversations I have about shamanic wisdom + ceremony is remarkable. There is something happening... and it's happening faster + faster! It is an ascending cycle of the... GREAT YEAR!

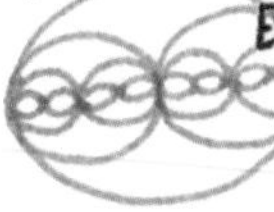

Everything occurs in cycles... and cycles within cycles of greater cycles. The cycle of day + night and the turn of the seasons are easy ones to grasp. Many cultures also speak of the importance of much longer cycles. This is a "Great Year," completing one cycle of the equinoxes approximately every 26,000 years. But what if all meant something much more than the slow wobble of the Earth's axis? Greek mythology tells us of the Golden, Silver, Bronze + Iron ages... Hindu texts speak of the four-age cycles known as Yugas. And the ancient Mayans had 13 different calendars for tracking different cycles of time. The longest was an era of 13 Baktuns, or 5,128 years.
(144,000 days x 13 Baktuns = 5,128 years)
And multiplied by 5 = GREAT YEAR

Perhaps so many cultures tracked these long cycles because of our tendency to forget who we are... these calendars were like setting a COSMIC ALARM CLOCK

It's time to awaken again to our true nature. We've come out of the descending ages where we fell asleep and only believed our 5 senses.. Where we stand now is a restructuring of WHO you are from the inside out emerging from our chrysalis. This journey through your Cosmic Journal is an evolution of your next greatest work. We are awaiting your addition to the majestic tapestry of the Universe, to sign your TRUE name as the artist. The "end" is really just the beginning again of your journey back to the stars...

13.0.0.0.0
Dec. 21, 2012
11:11 UT

What's Next?

What started as an interesting experiment turned into something much bigger than I could have imagined. In fact I never even intended to publish this work; it was just for me.

Originally, I set a challenge for myself to create a new journal entry every day for 108 days. I wasn't really sure I could do it because of my travel and other commitments. That meant more than a few nights where I didn't get to bed until 4 AM. Actually, I remember one night I fell asleep while drawing, and my pen slipped. I had already spent all this time illustrating a picture and I made a "mistake" on the quote. ACK! But that "screwup" turned into an even more powerful entry. I got goose bumps as I wrote it...

This kind of MAGIC, those signs + synchronicities I spoke of, started happening all around me. It was uncanny. Friends saw my pages and were astounded as the "RIGHT" message they needed to hear fell out for them. It made sense since I created the Cosmic Journal for myself to Remember my own role here...

((To Catalyze the Catalysts ... You.))

My ultimate intention is for this journal to be a homing beacon, attracting the individuals who somehow "accidentally" stumbled onto this guide to realize they are one of the 1,000 suns – who can each light 1000 It only requires your Effortless Effort... SUNS! Fulfill your Destiny as part of this new ascending AGE.

ARE YOU READY?

If the Cosmic Journal has triggered something in your heart and your soul, come explore further with us at:

Cosmic Journal . com / one

* See Bonus entries + new pages
* Get resources + training for your own Cosmic Journal
* Connect with other allies + Cosmic Catalysts
* Fully customized versions of the Cosmic Journal for groups + communities are available

About the Author

YANIK SILVER has been called a Cosmic Catalyst, a Maverick Mischief-maker, and a Galactic Goofball. He redefines how business is played in the 21st century at the intersection of evolutionary growth, impact, and fun. Yanik is the author of Evolved Enterprise and the founder of Maverick1000, a global collective of visionary entrepreneurs making a serious difference in the world, without taking themselves too seriously. In fact, it's not unusual to find him dressed as a lemur, a showgirl, or even in matching mermaid tails with Sir Richard Branson.

Yanik believes we all have our own "Cosmic Alarm Clock" that goes off at exactly the right time to fulfill our destiny of greatness. It starts as a whisper, a small voice that gets louder and louder until you either answer it or hit snooze. He has spent his life exploring that connection of head, heart, and highest purpose . . . with his colored pens in hand. It might have all started when he snuck out at the age of 5 to buy markers—only to catch the wrong bus home and end up at the police station. (Undaunted, his love of doodling and exploring still continue to this day!)

Websites: www.yaniksilver.com and
www.CosmicJournal.com

We hope you enjoyed this Hay House book. If you'd like to receive our online catalog featuring additional information on Hay House books and products, or if you'd like to find out more about the Hay Foundation, please contact:

Hay House, Inc., P.O. Box 5100, Carlsbad, CA 92018-5100
(760) 431-7695 or (800) 654-5126
(760) 431-6948 (fax) or (800) 650-5115 (fax)
www.hayhouse.com® • www.hayfoundation.org

———

Published in Australia by: Hay House Australia Pty. Ltd.,
18/36 Ralph St., Alexandria NSW 2015
Phone: 612-9669-4299 • *Fax:* 612-9669-4144
www.hayhouse.com.au

Published in the United Kingdom by: Hay House UK, Ltd.,
The Sixth Floor, Watson House, 54 Baker Street, London W1U 7BU
Phone: +44 (0)20 3927 7290 • *Fax:* +44 (0)20 3927 7291
www.hayhouse.co.uk

Published in India by: Hay House Publishers India,
Muskaan Complex, Plot No. 3, B-2, Vasant Kunj, New Delhi 110 070
Phone: 91-11-4176-1620 • *Fax:* 91-11-4176-1630
www.hayhouse.co.in

———

ACCESS NEW KNOWLEDGE.
ANYTIME. ANYWHERE.

Learn and evolve at your own pace
with the world's leading experts.

www.hayhouseU.com